the complete

fashion sketchbook

Martin Dawber

BATSFORD

Below:
Rosa Ng (2011)

First published in the United Kingdom in 2013 by
Batsford, 10 Southcombe Street, London W14 0RA
An imprint of Anova Books Company Ltd

Copyright © Batsford 2013
Text © Martin Dawber 2013
Illustrations © as credited on the relevant pages

ISBN 978 1 84994 114 3
A CIP catalogue record for this book is available from
the British Library.

10 9 8 7 6 5 4 3 2 1

Reproduction by Mission Production Ltd, Hong Kong
Printed and bound by 1010 Printing International Ltd,
China

Dedication

'The hardest thing to see is what is in front of your eyes.'
Johann Wolfgang von Goethe (1749–1832)

This book is for Carole

the bones of belief.
"on the beautiful dead we rest"

Above
Jousianne Propp (2012)
'Technoligion', Graduate
Collection 2012.

Contents

Foreword

On my Foundation Course at Hertfordshire College of Art and Design in 1987 I encountered the idea of a sketchbook for the very first time. Up until then I never gave a sketchbook a second thought – perhaps I had never heard of one. I was never a child who drew, sketched or was encouraged to do so. The idea of a sketchbook was so new to me and I had no idea of how important it was to become for the rest of my life.

My tutors on Foundation were always going on about how I had to have a sketchbook – how it would form my ideas and give me a place to put everything down. Being young and 18 and not really wanting to do anything, I didn't keep a sketchbook throughout the year. I was not alone – many of my fellow students just didn't do it. We rebelled. We just wanted to do large-scale paintings and sculptures.

Towards the end of my Foundation Course we were required to present our work. Each student had their own booth where we set up our finished artwork, portfolios, sketches and photographs. Our tutors told us we were also required to display the 10–12 sketchbooks that we had been keeping throughout the year.

I thought 'F**k! I only have one sketch book half full!'. So, in order to fulfill the requirements, I began what was to be one of the most intense experiences of my student life. I sketched, I added paint, dirt, pieces of paper, glue, seeds, fish heads, footprints, potato prints, photos, etchings – even a doll's head. I sketched with my left hand and I sketched with my right hand. At the end of the week I had finished my sketchbooks – all 12, filled to the brim, busting at the seams, overflowing with ideas with everything I could think of – appropriate or otherwise.

But something kind of magical happened along the way. I learned the importance of the sketchbook and how significant it is to my process of designing.

Today, over 20 years later, I'm always working in five to six sketchbooks at any one time. They are always with me – they go where I go. I sketch a lot while travelling, especially while flying. Time is suspended when I'm flying and it's easy for me to let my imagination open up. Many of the collections for Duckie Brown have started on the 8am flight from New York to London.

For Duckie Brown, each season is formulated in a Moleskine plain paper sketchbook – they are easy to carry and I can take them everywhere.

For the last eleven years – that's 22 collections – each one has started with writing in my sketchbook. Writing has become very important to my process, though it never was at school. I'm not a writer – that's not my strength. I write words down first – the words express what I see in my imagination. I write down what I think the collection is about. Every collection is always based on the lives we lead and what is around us at that moment. So there are the words, and these lead to my ideas … and from there comes the first sketches and the collection starts to take form. What come first are always my bad sketches and I've learned that's fine. I only do a sketchbook for one person, and one person only, and that's me. I show very few people my sketchbooks.

As the sketches progress, they become more specific and eventually the sketches become what the collection will look like. It doesn't happen by magic. I might do ten or 20 or 100 sketches before I hit the right one – the one I know it feels right – and then I know I'm on to something and I can see where the collection is going. I'm on a roll. I have a clear vision. My sketches are quick and very loose. From there I enlarge the best sketches from my sketchbook and trace over them with a pencil on to a Bienfang marker sketchbook and the process of the finished fashion illustrations begins.

Once that's done they go up on the wall to inform everything we do for that season's collection. Often my sketches are done almost like a run of the show but in sketch form. At the same time the fabrics are being ordered and when delivered I lean them up against the sketches. Most recently I've started to do collage work with my sketches. I place fabric on the sketches and so they become complete looks.

Everyone has to find their version of what a sketchbook means for them. It's so very personal. No one can tell you how to do it – you really have to discover it for yourself. But when you do – it's magic.

Steven Cox
New York City, 2012

<u>Below:</u>
Rosa Ng (2011)

Introduction

In an age of smart phones and iPads it might appear out of kilter for contemporary fashion creatives still to cling to a physical journal or sketchbook in which to assemble their thoughts and ideas. It is like continuing to work in pounds, shillings and pence when everyone else has moved over to decimal currency. Yet for most, if it came to the burning-building test, it is always these very items that they would rescue at all costs. Why? What is it that makes these throwbacks to pre-digital climes so valuable in an age where information is literally at one's fingertips?

At face value these books can look like a riot of unrelated scraps of visual DNA that seem to be bursting – often quite literally – out of the confines of the actual pages of the book. There isn't anything to anchor the sketchbook to a uniform appearance. They can vary in size from small pocketbook Moleskines through to bulky A2 dimensions. They can be pre-bought or self-manufactured. Some designers prefer to work on single pages and assemble them at a later date. Others might regard the name 'sketchbook' as something of a misnomer, since the contents far exceed the traditional idea of a book primarily filled with sketches or drawings. In fact, they are also known under other labels: logbooks, visual journals, dossiers, handbooks, design diaries, creative-process journals, notebooks, scrapbooks and thinking books. This diversity in both the appearance and name for a sketchbook is a pointer to its very personal nature and identity.

> 'My sketchbook is a witness of what I am experiencing, scribbling things whenever they happen.'
> Vincent van Gogh
> (1853–1890)

On first acquaintance the contents of a sketchbook can appear more like palmistry and you'd need a fortune-teller to interpret their meaning. By default each designer will have employed his or her own unique personal language, using a private vocabulary that usually comes across as more intuitive than planned. However, don't judge a fashion sketchbook by its cover! Despite their initial dense appearance, these books are capable of representing the considered and selected visual articulation of each designer's thoughts and intentions. This is where a designer collates information that will eventually point the way through a design task towards an exciting and innovative conclusion. They are industriously assembled, using layer after layer of assorted nuggets of information that are often only recognized as potentially valuable by the designer. They don't necessarily adhere to a strict pattern of purpose, and although every page will be important, they will not necessarily be in any sequential order. They permit all manner of self-indulgent tendencies that would be frowned upon elsewhere. Sketchbooks are places where mistakes can and should be made. They need

Left
Jade Elizabeth Hannam (2012)

Opposite
Hannah Dowds (2010–12)

neck with opens.
shaped
sleeves.

feathers.

fited shapes.

GREY

Beryl Grey, a dancer with an easy classical te
magnificent line and great warmth. She made he
a première danseuse during the war when, at a
age she was entrusted with many leading roles b
classical and modern repertoires. Her height, un
undoubted handicap, espe

Loewe

Valentino

Jaeger London

Jaeger   Zacposen

...oh y

fox is snugly curled in an ou
over Matter (2006), a small
of Venison in London is feat
"Mythologies," on view from

to be regularly updated and kept fresh by the repeated addition of newly garnered material. Sketchbooks empower fashion designers to play around with and unravel their personal cache of visual information – without the hang-up of a polished finished appearance – and to rehearse and experiment with the best methods of working through their ideas. *Complete Fashion Sketchbook* will help all aspiring fashion creatives to enjoy exploring the varied techniques and methods of keeping their own fashion sketchbook. It will exemplar exciting ways to catalogue design concepts and to solve problems. It won't provide all the answers – that is up to you, the reader – but it will show you inventive ways to identify, source and compile fashion research. This will increase your own creativity and imagination in order to present your own findings in a visually stimulating and original sketchbook. This book is not intended to be prescriptive. Don't feel there is an obligation to imitate – a sketchbook should always demonstrate your own personality and individualism. *Complete Fashion Sketchbook* is intended to set you off on a uniquely personal journey of discovery. You will be signposted to all the necessary ingredients to enable you to confront the challenges that face you and to strengthen your talents and self-confidence when working in a sketchbook. It requires commitment, but the personal gains will be rewards in themselves.

Fashion sketchbooks are all about design as process rather than any final product. They are entirely concerned with the exploration and engagement of their subject and follow a variety of procedures for enquiry. A fashion sketchbook provides the perfect medium to go deep into the procedures of design without the worry of ever using it as a finished endpoint. A designer won't necessarily be judged on his sketchbooks, but they certainly play a vital role in underpinning the activity of design.

The sketchbook has always provided invaluable insight into the working methods of artists and designers – both contemporary and historical. It is like reading their guarded private diaries and this protection makes their intimate visual secrets even more appealing. This previously locked private world has increasingly been gaining recognition on its own terms. The once restricted view from behind the scenes has been opened out and the sketchbook is now out on show. Progressively more and more art galleries and museums are using sketchbooks in their displays – some even mounting sketchbook-only exhibitions.

The Brooklyn Art Library in New York continues to gather and archive its unique collection of sketchbooks by contemporary artists, and New York's Museum of Modern Art houses a vast array of rare artists' sketchbooks past and present within its Department of Drawing. American realist painter, Irwin Greenberg (1922–2009), once commented 'An artist is a sketchbook with a person attached.'

There are regular conferences and gatherings exclusively about sketchbooks – The Moment of Privacy Has Passed (Lincoln School of Art and Design, UK) and the Ready, Set, Sketch! Symposium (Faculty of Fine Arts of the University of Lisbon, Portugal) both drew worldwide contributors and audiences. Back in the UK, The Rabley Art Project operates a national award solely for artists' sketchbooks.

One of the most valued historical examples of an artist's sketchbook is the collection of notebooks left behind by Leonardo da Vinci (1452–1519) following his death. Subsequently sold off, page by page, they were re-assembled by their subject matter as codices by Pompeo Leoni (c.1533–1608) in 1630. They famously employ his left-hand mirror shorthand to keep his jottings private and to protect his prototypes. In 1994 Microsoft founder Bill Gates (b.1955) purchased the 72-page *Codex Leicester*, which catalogues Leonardo's theories on astronomy, for an estimated $30.8 million. It now holds the record as the world's most valuable second-hand manuscript.

As with all creative industries, a fashion sketchbook is recognized as the essential repository for sourced information and the sounding board to test out ideas. However, unlike some technical blueprints, the fashion sketchbook is not concluded at the start of the design process. It is constantly updated throughout, and operates like an ongoing visual diary to log the designer's progression, and to chart their design development. Although there are no concrete rules, or magic recipes, for generating a sketchbook – in a class of 60 students there can be as many methods of compiling the information as actual students – there are certain characteristics that are necessary for the gathering together of the information and for articulating these findings towards a meaningful conclusion.

A good sketchbook should be brimming over with visual imagery (both primary and secondary) and be capable of evidencing both the passion and the creative imagination of the designer. It is essential that the sketchbook demonstrates a designer's ability to develop an idea and run with it through a process of personal investigation and evaluation. American artist Robert Motherwell (1915–91) said 'For me, the sketchbooks are more like a secret and wholly spontaneous *jeu d'esprit* and some of them I like as much as anything I have ever done.'

So, where do you start? The sketchbook might be to support a specialist task that already has prescriptive or client requirements. It might be an opportunity to test out some new ideas and concepts personally: a visit to an ancient cathedral might suggest directions for shape and silhouette or watching a sunset over the ocean might conjure up an original colour story. What comes first in the design process is different every time you begin a task. You will need to collect all the facts in your sketchbook, but the order might change depending on your inspiration.

CHAPTER 1

Research: areas to investigate

'If you steal from one author, it's plagiarism;
if you steal from many, it's research.'

Wilson Mizner (1876-1933)

The word 'research' often suggests scientific facts and values. It is usually undertaken over a long period of time and is tested and then tested again until it is fit for purpose. How can a fashion designer use research to benefit his or her designs when they don't deal in facts but use creativity as the conduit for their investigations and relish the unknown and unimaginable as their output? They are also usually working against the clock or an impossible deadline. So how can it be called 'research'?

Simple really – for a designer, research relies upon intuition, ingenuity and imagination.

All designers are by their nature inquisitive people: they have a curiosity about life and a thirst for information that is best quenched by undertaking research. Research will always form the lifeblood of any design process. Insufficient investigation at the onset of a project will inevitably result in not having enough fuel to feed your imagination later on. You need to cast a wide net to trawl lots of useful information and ideas. Most designers tend to chronicle their environment on a need-to-know basis – pulling in appropriate reference as it is needed. Don't just accumulate information like an avid philatelist – quantity also needs to be matched to purpose.

Sustaining a project through the design stages requires a lot of intellectual stamina and creativity, which in turn relies upon a constant infusion of design data that can be accessed and analyzed as required. The more data you harvest upfront and store for future reference, the better you will be equipped when you start to employ your research.

Surface plunder is all well and good, but you will also need to dig deeper and unearth the new and unknown. The richer the treasure, the better it will expand your horizons and guide you to something new and original. Above all it is essential that you articulate your passion for the subject throughout your research.

The fashion industry has a unique reputation within the design world for its unashamed ability to feed from itself and seemingly be applauded for it – where would fast-fashion retail be without the trickle-down effect of the latest re-invented catwalk trends with each new delivery? Conversely, street fashion applies a 'bubble-up' effect by generating an impact as an identifiable trend, usually through exposure in the media, before being voraciously assimilated into high couture.

<u>Above</u>
Julie Campbell (2011)
Research should always be untaken as a personal investigation into areas that directly interest you, so that you can acquire the crucial reference necessary to support your individuality as a fashion designer.

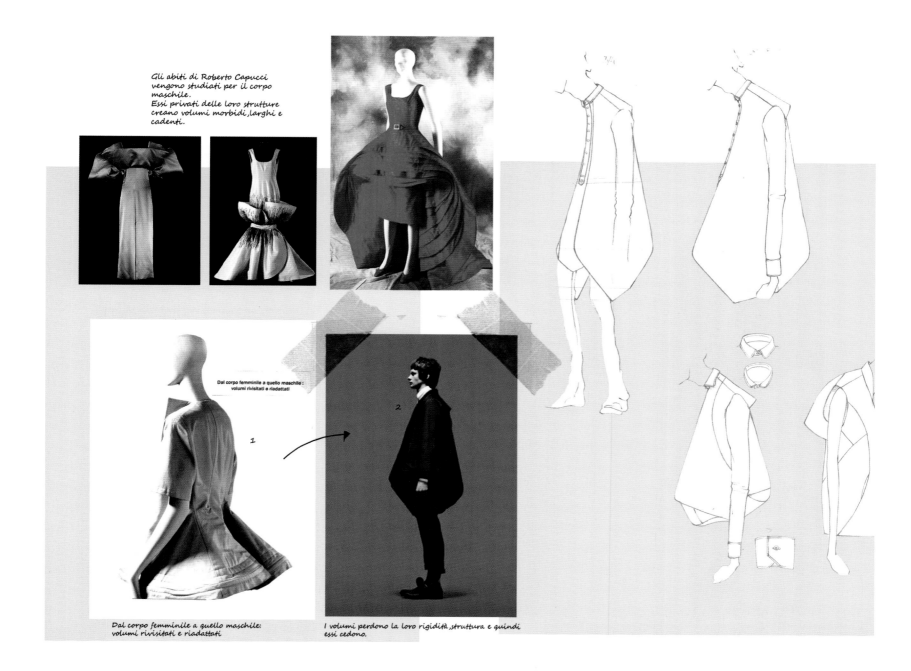

Gli abiti di Roberto Capucci vengono studiati per il corpo maschile.
Essi privati delle loro strutture creano volumi morbidi, larghi e cadenti.

Dal corpo femminile a quello maschile : volumi rivisitati e riadattati

1

2

Dal corpo femminile a quello maschile: volumi rivisitati e riadattati

I volumi perdono la loro rigidità, struttura e quindi essi cedono.

Although trademark protection exists within the fashion industry there is very little intellectual property protection (other than the protection awarded to the actual fabric, which is not usually created by the fashion designer) since apparel *per se* (along with food and furniture) is considered too utilitarian to qualify. This lack of copyright or patent protection on the physical pieces of a garment (a neckline, a sleeve, etc.) requires designers to look outside the technical components of fashion for their trend direction and inspiration.

<u>Above</u>
Filomena Cavallaro (2011)
Looking at past designers from a 21st-century perspective is a way to expand your knowledge and develop your own garment design concepts. French writer Marcel Proust (1871-1922) said 'The real voyage of discovery consists not in seeking new landscapes, but in having new eyes.'

So where do you start?

Most often there will be a problem that you have been asked to solve. This might be a design assignment set by a tutor as part of your coursework or a competition brief that has specific requirements. In industry the most frequent task will be designing the next collection.

You will usually have detailed objectives and your research is the first step towards achieving those requirements. Don't fall into the trap of thinking too literally about your answers. Stepping away from the subject allows you to approach it with new eyes and an open mind. Always be on the lookout for an alternative route towards your goal and don't be seduced by the first things that you find. Try out unconventional means of obtaining your information. Be curious. Taking a chance is a vital element of the creative process. Remember that if it's easy to locate then it has probably already been found and used before.

Fashion will always be difficult to pin down and can never be dealt with in pure isolation. It is almost mystical in its intricate multi-layering and ever-changeable disposition. This is where a sketchbook becomes a vital and stimulating piece of the fashion designer's kitbag. It is the repository for all your findings and it will help to clarify your ideas by pointing your imagination towards future developments and conclusions.

There are several basic ingredients that need to be borne in mind when you set out to design anything. These are known as the Principles and Elements of Design. These factors can determine the aesthetic value or success of any design outcome. They are the blueprints that uphold the traditional ideals that underlie the whole field of design and represent its basic axioms and truths. A good, or an equally bad design, will apply most if not all of these values. They are categorized or adhered to depending on the specialist design field. Within fashion design there are four basic elements: shape and form, line, colour and texture. There are also five fundamental principles for the fashion designer to consider: proportion and scale, balance, unity, rhythm and emphasis.

For the conscientious fashion designer it is obviously important to be aware of what constitutes a good design even if in the end it will be their intention to challenge the system. Rules can only be broken once you know what they are.

For the purpose of your fashion sketchbook the following generic headings form the basic starting blocks for any enquiry into fashion:

1. Colour
2. Silhouette
3. Line and balance
4. Shape, form and texture.

Left
Matteo Busanna (2011)
Burberry Project
Try to take an alternative viewpoint towards
your investigations and don't be too obvious
in its translation. Alexander McQueen (1969-
2010) said, 'You've got to know the rules
to break them. That's what I'm here for, to
demolish the rules but to keep the tradition.'

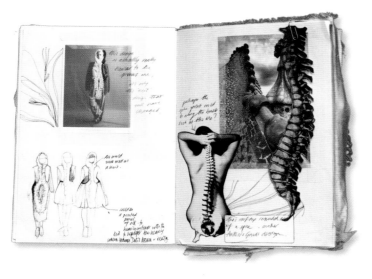

Left
Hâf Evans (2012)

Right
Talisa Almonte (2012)

Below
Jessica Larcombe (2012)
Keeping an open mind when researching will give a richer resource to drawn upon when you move towards design development. Global trend forecaster and creative director of the Doneger Group David Wolfe (b.1941) said, 'When I ride the subway to work, I'm doing research. I never stop.'

Colour: the ever-changing palette of fashion

'He who knows how to appreciate colour relationships,
the influence of one colour on another, their contrasts and dissonances,
is promised an infinitely diverse imagery.'

Sonia Delauney (1885-1979)

Colour is a crucial tool for anyone attempting to design within the fashion industry. Colour does not operate in isolation within the design process and its importance cannot be overlooked. It is usually the visual impact of colour that first appeals to any customer. Forecasting the latest colour trends is an important business because the look and style of fashion changes more rapidly that for any other of the design areas. It is key for the forecaster to combine a personal knowledge of fashion design, culture and history with consumer preferences. Projections about the colour palettes for forthcoming seasons are provided as indicators to designers. They predict the rise and fall of essential colours each season.

The American group Pantone, Inc. is a market leader in the communication of colour from the designer via the manufacturer and retailer down to the customer. The PANTONE Textile Color System ® is used by designers worldwide when selecting and specifying colours and consists of over 1,932 colours available as both paper and cotton fabric samples. They also issue a twice yearly PANTONE VIEW Colour Planner ® that provides seasonal colour direction and inspiration for the designer to access 24 months in advance of the intended season. The fashion and textiles industry usually adopts a two-year window in order for the yarn producers to dye up the new season's colours well in advance of the actual selling season.

Colour will always be subjective. Colour appeals to the senses (as with music or food) and doesn't follow any rules or objective criteria to explain our preferences. Personal preferences, cultural backgrounds, and associated memories can all prompt contrasting opinions as to the value and meaning of a particular colour. While wearing black for a funeral may be considered *de rigeur* in Europe, in China and parts of Africa white is the accepted colour of mourning, as is yellow in Egypt. The tradition of dressing baby girls in pink and boys in blue doesn't hold sway in Belgium where it is the opposite, while in Bermuda and Japan pink is also regarded as a very masculine colour.

Below
Philippa
Jenkins
(2010)

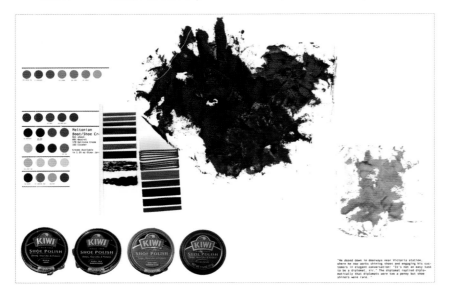

In the world of fashion colour can make or break success. Would the universal acceptance of denim jeans have taken off if they had originally been red or green? Would the 'little black dress' have been as seductively flattering if it had been christened the 'little yellow dress'?

To meet consumer demand most retail brands will always offer a choice of colours for the same item. Knowing how to mix and balance colour is therefore crucial to the success of any fashion designer's output. The Director of Corporate Marketing at PANTONE, Giovanni Marra, said 'Color inspires us in our everyday lives while influencing our moods, feelings and ultimately our buying decisions. The proper use of color in design should not be underestimated as it is critical to any product or campaign success.'

The names of colours have increasingly filtered into everyday speech. Although there seems to be little regard for their symbolic meanings, there is usually some historical or cultural reference to explain their (sometimes curious) usage. While everyone is familiar with the content of a 'blue' joke, no one ever wants to be handed their 'pink' slip, or have their most valued purchase thought of as a 'white' elephant. Equally, everyone would like to be given the red-carpet treatment, but would hate to be caught red-handed.

Colour can also use its own inbuilt language to inform and direct you in your daily life in a multitude of ways: the colour red means 'danger' and 'stop' while green means 'safe' and 'go' at most traffic lights across the world; gold, silver and bronze are colours that represent achievement; a white flag is a sign of surrender and a white feather symbolizes cowardice; financially it is always more preferable to be in the black rather than in the red.

The combinations appear endless and sometimes even contradictory.

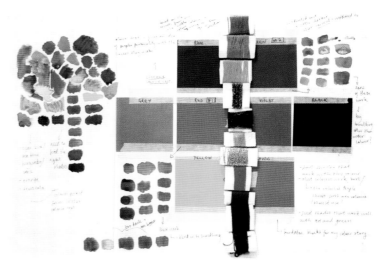

Above
Emily Rickard (2012)

Below
Rebecca Dring (2012)
Each fashion designer explores colour in a way that is not only compatible with their own personal design aesthetic but will also heighten the message that they want to express through their garments.

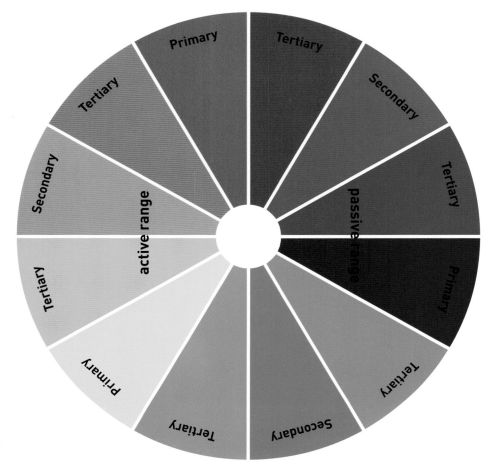

Right
A colour wheel is a circular
representation of colours
arranged according to their
chromatic relationship. The
wheel can also be divided into
ranges that are considered either
visually active or passive.

Colour theory has been thoroughly researched and documented throughout the centuries and most of today's designers turn to the colour wheel as a guide when selecting and using colour. This is a rudimentary version of the colour spectrum pulled into a circle that shows a progression of equidistant, radiating coloured bands. Each of the pure spectrum colours on the wheel (identified as hues) can be adjusted by tinting (through the addition of white), shading (through the addition of black) or toning (through the addition of both white and black).

The first colour circle was developed by Sir Isaac Newton (1642–1727) in 1666 to document the chromatic relationship and natural progression from one colour to the next. In 1810, Johann Wolfgang von Goethe allocated psychological effects and meanings to different colours by dividing them up into plus and minus groupings. Bauhaus tutor and painter Johannes Itten (1888–1967), published *The Art of Colour* in 1961. He modified existing theories and devised a new colour wheel that was made up of 12 hues. It is Itten's colour sphere that still forms the basis of colour analysis classes taught at art schools today and is adhered to by contemporary designers. Itten said 'Colour is life, for a world without colour seems dead. As a flame produces light, light produces colour. As intonation lends colour to the spoken word, colour lends spiritually realized sound to form.'

In simple terms most colours fall within three basic colour groupings of primary, secondary or tertiary colours. Red, yellow and blue are the three primary pigment colours that have the unique property that they cannot be produced by mixing other colours together. However, within the printing industry, the three primary colours are magenta, cyan and yellow. The three secondary colours of green, orange and purple, are created by mixing equal quantities from any of the two primary colours. The six tertiary colours are produced when a primary and adjacent secondary colour are combined (e.g.: yellow-orange, red-orange, red-purple, blue-purple, blue-green and yellow-green).

The colours positioned opposite one another on a colour wheel are known as complementary colours because they work well when used together, as do those located adjacent to one another, which are known as analogous colours. Vincent van Gogh's *Sunflowers* is a perfect example of the use of analogous colours, where the related orange, yellow-orange and yellows within the composition complement one another perfectly. When three equally spaced colours around the colour wheel are selected in a suitable combination, these are known as triad colours.

Monochromatic colours are achieved when a single colour is graded into varying shades of itself, either by darkening or lightening the original hue, or by increasing or reducing its saturation. You will be familiar with this sequence if you have ever used colour cards when trying to mix paint at a hardware store. There are groupings of warm colours.

Red: an intense colour suggestive of sunsets and blazing fires that can also indicate love as well as danger and anger.

Orange: always associated with the fruit is not only suggestive of health and wellbeing but can also reflect the seasons.

Yellow: the colour of sunshine also has associations with a positive outlook.

Cooler colours are more restrained than warm colours.

Green: although representative of nature and renewal it is also capable of suggesting envy and jealousy.

Blue: the colour of the sky and the sea is suggestive of tranquility and stability but also has religious connotations as in depictions of the Virgin Mary.

Purple: has immediate associations with nobility and royalty but in lighter hues can also reflect romance.

Where does this leave black and white? Unfortunately both of these colours are not as easy to quantify. In certain circles it is even argued that they are not really colours at all. The absence of any colours on a computer screen would be interpreted as black; but if you were reading a book or magazine, the white background to the text would also be decoded by your brain as blank or empty: two colours – same result.

Physically mixing all three primary colours together gives a black colour (of sorts), and although you cannot mix any of the other colours to make white, it is still not acknowledged as a primary colour. Confused? Don't be. Just remember that whether 'true' colours or not, black and white should be freely exploited along with the rest in any exploration of colour.

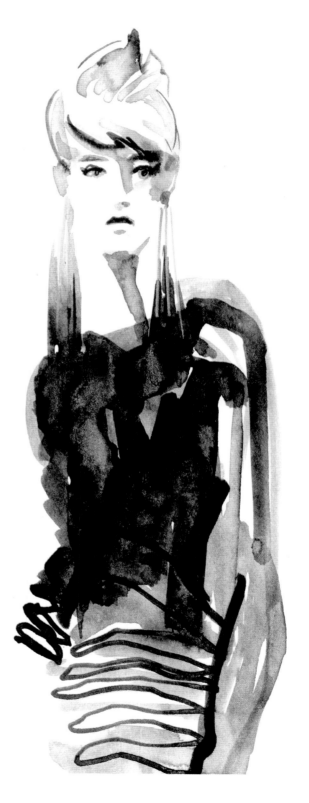

Right
Meagan Morrison (2011)
Although Edouard Manet (1832-83) declared that 'Black is not a colour', the fashion world has persistently closed its ears. Ever since Coco Chanel (1883-1971) and Christian Dior (1905-57) established its appeal, the colour black has been universally upheld as the ultimate in fashionable chic. Today the term 'the new black' is often used to express the latest colour trend.

Here is a quick summary of the main colour associations:

Red: Passion, Love, Urgency, Excitement, Strength, Violence, Anger, Danger

Orange: Energy, Balance, Warmth, Health, Happiness, Vitality, Flamboyance

Yellow: Optimism, Joy, Happiness, Hope, Sunshine, Cowardice, Sickness

Green: Nature, Growth, Youth, Fertility, Vigour, Jealousy, Envy, Nausea

Blue: Trust, Coolness, Peace, Responsible, Cleanliness, Sadness, Spirituality

Purple: Magic, Ceremony, Dignity, Royalty, Wealth, Arrogance, Decadence

Black: Mystery, Elegance, Night, Evil, Unhappiness, Depression

White: Purity, Cleanliness, Truth, Heroism, Kindness, Innocence, Neutrality

Fake Flowers Never Fade

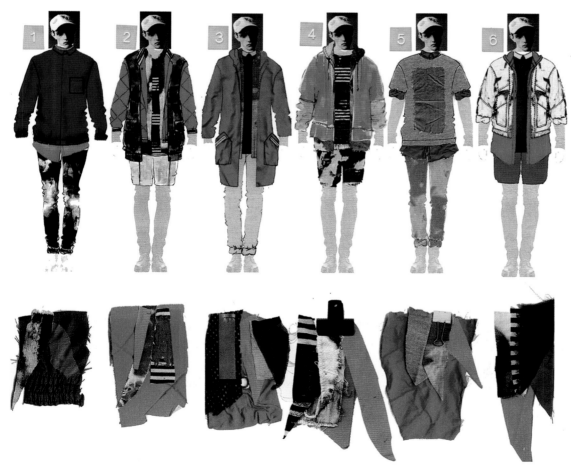

Below
Georgia Smith (2012)
Colour and fabric choice will always go hand in hand. A wide choice in both can easily dilute the overall impact of your designs and become too chaotic and over-busy – a case of 'not seeing the wood for the trees'. Restricting yourself to a narrower palette within a limited fabric selection can become repetitive and will demand more attention in the construction of individual garments in order to provide variety and interest. Balancing colour and fabrication is necessary in order to secure the best from your overall design concept. By combining a dominant core colour with a range of supporting accent colours, it is possible to establish a pleasing overall colour story that both binds together and provides diversity within an inclusive palette choice.

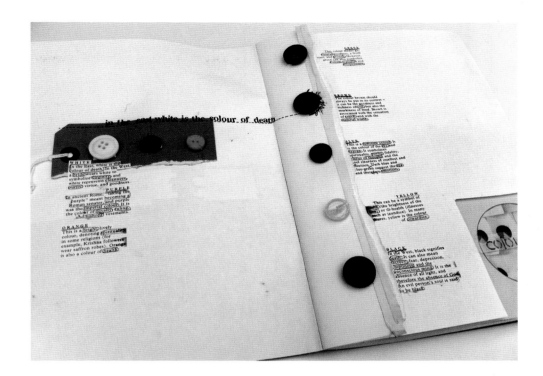

Opposite
Talisa Almonte
(2012)

Above
Samme Williams
(2011)

Below
Rebecca Head
(2012)

The stimulus for selecting a colour palette will ultimately be down to a designer's personal reaction to his or her research and design concept. It might be as simple as a literal response to a dramatic landscape or environment that is in keeping with the mood or season of the intended collection. Colour can also be used to instigate social comment or dramatically usurp the known with a radical reinterpretation of the obvious. Whatever the intention, you should always take full advantage of the added value that colour can bring to your designs and never underestimate its potential. It is imperative that you always allow sufficient time to test out and evaluate different combinations, proportions and balances of colour within your designs. Colour unites the whole design process - get it wrong and it is difficult to readjust at a later stage without going all the way back to the drawing board.

Sketchbook task

Word association with colour palettes

Have you ever wondered how the increasingly obscure and elaborate names for some of today's colour and shade charts originate? It doesn't matter if it's household paint or a nail polish, colour names are often very ambiguous – Waterlily Blush, Nectar Jewels, Mercury Shower – all are difficult to bring to the mind's eye just by their name alone. This is an attempt to 're-invent' the colour – to keep it fresh and up to date.

'What's in a name? That which we call a rose By any other name would smell as sweet.'

Romeo and Juliet, William Shakespeare (1564–1616)

Most colour forecasting is presented in colour stories – each colour palette is offered with its own history and context for its selection and name. Place yourself in the forecaster's shoes with this fun exercise, by organizing and naming a simple colour story and palette.

1. Think of a generic heading for your proposed colour story.

2. Then write out ten descriptive words or adjectives associated with your colour-story heading.

3. Now combine each of the descriptors with a colour that you associate with your colour palette heading and re-brand each colour with its new identity. Use two words for each colour. Previously unrelated words are a better option for new names – when combined they shouldn't offer anything that is instantly recognizable and already in your memory banks.

4. Finally, match each of your newly named colours to a suitably suggestive image.

5. Add the conclusions to your sketchbook.

BRAVE
+
BLUE
=

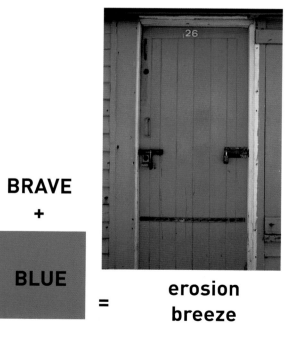

erosion
breeze

CALM
+
STONE
=

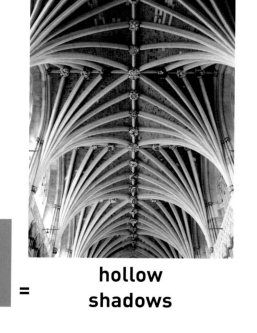

hollow
shadows

Here are some suggestions for colour stories and likely descriptors:

EMOTIONS	WEATHER	TASTE	MOVIES	APPEARANCES
Angry	Foggy	Bitter	Adventure	Beautiful
Calm	Frosty	Delicious	Comical	Clean
Embarrassed	Hot	Fruity	Epic	Drab
Gentle	Icy	Greasy	Historical	Fancy
Happy	Overcast	Yummy	Horrific	Glamorous
Lazy	Rainy	Mellow	Musical	Magnificent
Mysterious	Stormy	Peppery	Romantic	Plain
Nervous	Sunny	Spicy	Violent	Sparkling
Scary	Sweltering	Sticky	Wacky	Unsightly
Worried	Windy	Yummy	Western	Wide-eyed

HAPPY

+

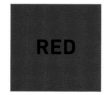 **RED** **= cinnabar fever**

Sketchbook task

'A large rose-tree stood near the entrance of the garden: the roses growing on it were white, but there were three gardeners at it, busily painting them red. Alice thought this a very curious thing …'

Alice's Adventures in Wonderland, Lewis Carroll (1832-98)

Colour swap

What happens when something that is distinguished by its colour has a makeover and appears in an alternate colourway? Would you still be tempted to eat a banana if it was lavender blue, or swim in the sea if it was blood red? What if trees had pink leaves and fire engines were painted yellow?

1. Using non-garment imagery, try to select a series of images that are recognizable by their colour: it could be a desert scene, a frozen wasteland, a New York yellow cab, or even a bunch of carrots.Now set about changing its natural colour palette. What method will you use to swap around the colour? You could paint over the image, mark out and attach replacement coloured film to the image, or use computer software to adjust the colour of a scanned image. Don't restrict yourself to just one alteration. Think of Andy Warhol's (1928–87) screen prints and how your reaction to and opinion of the object alters due to the rearrangement of blocks of colour.

2. Now carry out the same task using a fashion-related item as your stating point. What would a goth look like wearing baby blue? How would a bride's white dress appear if it were decked out in shades of fluorescent orange? Repeat your colour swaps to build up a grid of readjusted colour stories.

3. Include the results in your sketchbook.

Right
Because blue doesn't exist in any sizeable quantity in nature as a food colouring, it is often applied as a suppressant in dietary tests due to its unappetizing appearance.

Silhouette: the shape of fashion

'I try to push
the silhouette.
To change the
silhouette is to
change the thinking
of how we look.'

Alexander McQueen

A fashion silhouette is the overall shape that clothing and undergarments provide to enhance the natural body shape. This silhouette is created by the ingenuity of the garment's designer and the fabric employed to create it. Both the cut of the fabric and the outline of the clothes influence the optical illusion created when garments are worn. Silhouette can equally refer to the shape of a single garment or a combination of items that constitute a complete outfit.

The word silhouette originates from the name of the finance minister to Louis XV, Étienne de Silhouette (1709–67), who spent his retirement years cutting out paper profile portraits to decorate his home.

Because fashion is constantly changing, one of the key components of establishing a new look is the presentation of a different shape and silhouette each season. The silhouette of a garment is recognized before any other detailing becomes apparent.

| 1900–1909 | 1910–1919 | 1920–1929 | 1930–1939 | 1940–1949 |

As illustrated below, most periods in fashion retain their own distinct silhouette that instantly categorizes them as the culturally defining clothing of that era. A diverse range of silhouettes can be achieved by simply adjusting the waistline; shortening or lengthening sleeves, trousers or skirt lengths; or widening or narrowing shoulders, trousers or dresses. Twentieth-century trends in fashion can be easily pigeonholed via the observation of the decades' ever-changing silhouettes.

However, ten years is a long time in an industry that Oscar Wilde (1854–1900) described as 'a form of ugliness so intolerable that we have to alter it every six months', and silhouettes continually evolve across each progressive season. Although a century's generic silhouettes reveal an instant fashion snapshot (as below), each decade can also prove to be far more than just the sum of its parts when it comes to defining a look. Researching any era of the 20th century can be very informative and ultimately shows just how fickle the trends in fashion can be.

The 1970s is typical of the transient nature of fashion. Although the era began with a carry-over of the miniskirt, first introduced in the late 1960s, hemlines soon dropped to just below the knee, and later to 'midi' (mid-calf length) and then to 'maxi' (floor length); the previously sharp and clean silhouette was gradually replaced by fluid and unstructured garments inspired by peasant clothing. The flared silhouette exaggerated everything from 'A'-line outerwear, through to the empire-waisted dresses of the hippies, and later, the bellbottomed trousers or jumpsuits worn at the disco. The decade closed with the introduction of a style that eventually turned everything on its head – punk.

1950-1959   1960-1969   1970-1979   1980-1989   1990-1999

Modifications to the natural silhouette of the human frame have never been restricted to any one part. Across the centuries there isn't a single area of the body that hasn't fallen under the watchful eye of fashion as a potential focus for attention and exploitation. The pleated ruff collar is an example of a fashion statement that was equally important for both sexes. Expanding from a simple neckline embellishment, it eventually reached impractical cartwheel proportions as captured in the court portraits of the late 16th and early 17th centuries, and totally altered the shoulder silhouette.

One of the most instantly recognizable of all female silhouettes is that made by the Victorian crinoline. This famous bell-shaped silhouette framed by a hooped skirt began life as the farthingale in the fashionable Spanish court of the 16th century, and continued in popularity for nearly 300 years. It was later known as the biedermeier, crinoline or panier. The original hooped cages were made from bone or wood that were eventually replaced by steel and horsehair. In the mid-1800s the bustle took the place of the hoop skirt, creating a flatter-fronted silhouette by gathering all the fullness of the skirt at the back of the body. With the original intention of keeping the skirt's vast excesses of fabric from dragging across the floor, both the hooped skirt and the bustle made the waist look smaller and enhanced the profile of the bust, creating the S-line silhouette. However, the practical problems caused by dragging this volume and weight of fabric around, understandably caused an upsurge in reported back pain.

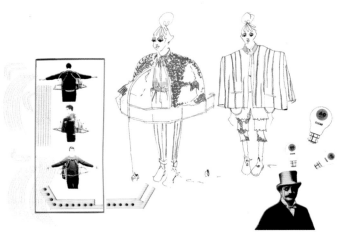

Above
Julia Krantz (2010)
'Shell'
While studying at HDK School of Design and Crafts in Gothenburg, Sweden, designer Julia Krantz used the principles of the crinoline for her collection of garments comprised of translucent fabrics draped over metal frames.
(Photography © Katrin Kirojood.)

Below
Rebecca Stant (2012)
A laser-cut plywood slot-system frame was devised by Manchester student, Rebecca Stant, to create an adjustable 'meccanoesque' frame to support the new garment silhouettes in her final collection.

Equally historically important in achieving a fashionable silhouette was the corset, which remained a fixture of a woman's wardrobe from the stiffened underbodices of the 15th century, through to the stays at the start of the 20th. However, suppressed waistlines have not always been similarly valued by all societies: in Japan, for instance, the broad *obi* sash worn to fasten the kimono had the effect of emphasizing the wearer's waist, rather than reducing it.

This obsession with stretching and shrinking the human form is understandable given that fashion designers only have so much to work with: at its most basic the human body consists simply of a trunk, two arms, two legs and a head. Over time every possible way of covering this singular frame have been tried and tested. For the contemporary fashion designer it remains as the continual problem for each season of where to go next: 'How can I dress the body in something that will be fresh, new and exciting?'

Although fashion designers use silhouette to flatter the human figure, they can sometimes be accused of giving scant regard to an individual's wellbeing as normal health considerations don't apply as they manipulate the body's natural outline to follow their own creative and imaginative contours. Culturally, as well as historically, suffering for fashion has been a corollary as style is often placed above comfort in the 'on-trend' stakes. It isn't just the reserve of professional models like Erin O'Connor (b.1978) who strutted down a Paris catwalk in 2001 wearing an Alexander McQueen outfit made entirely out of razor shells that left her hands cut to ribbons. The side effects of being in vogue over wearability can often lie much closer to reality for most would-be fashionistas.

French shoe designer, Christian Louboutin (b.1963), commented: 'High heels are pleasure with pain. If you can't walk in them, don't wear them.'

It is to the fashion designer's disadvantage that most designs in fashion are notoriously short lived. Most of the collections presented each season will be outmoded before each year-end. Trends can sometimes have almost overnight success – become a must-have following press or media coverage – but these fads fade out almost as quickly as they appeared. As Coco Chanel (1883–1971) expressed it, 'Fashion is made to become unfashionable'.

However, if a designer is lucky, every once in a while, a true 'classic' will be created, the silhouette of which will resurface in various manifestations time after time. A timeless classic is usually composed along clean, simple lines and has a clarity in both its silhouette and cut that give the garment instant appeal. The design, colour and fabrication synchronize together to suggest no other alternative scenario.

Notable 20th century fashion design classics have included the following:

The Burberry trench coat

Synonymous with class and style is the double-breasted, waterproof raincoat that Thomas Burberry (1835–1926) first designed back in 1901 as a trench coat for army officers. Traditional trenches come in three classic colours (khaki, beige or black). The raglan sleeve, gathered cuffs and D-ring shoulder straps help to endow the trench with its inimitable silhouette. It has the unique ability to appear both casual and professional at the same time. Hollywood stars as diverse as Humphrey Bogart (1899–1957), Greta Garbo (1905–90), Kim Novak (b.1933) and Meryl Streep (b.1949) helped to move it away from active service and gave it an alternative chic badge. The trench coat persists as a truly timeless classic with each generation putting a different spin on the basic template without altering its structural integrity. The trench remains as fashionable today as it was at the start of the 20th century. When the Duchess of Cambridge, Kate Middleton (b.1982), famously sported a Burberry trench coat on her highly publicized tour of Belfast in 2011, stocks of the trench both in stores and online in the UK, sold out within a single day.

heritage fabrics.

<u>Opposite, above</u>
Ross Williams (2012)
Technical flats help to explain
the continual fascination with
this by-product of America's
Wild West.

<u>Left</u>
Jousianne Propp
(2011)
Careful study of the
structure of heritage
garments will reveal
the ingredients that
have contributed to
their classic status.

<u>Opposite, below</u>
Olga Vokálová (2011)
A mood board reflecting on the
enduring attraction of classic
cut and styling in fashion's Hall
of Fame. As Ralph Lauren (b.1939)
explained 'I'm interested in
longevity, timelessness,
style - not fashion.'

Levi's® 501 jeans

The iconic Levi's® 501s are the best known of all jeans in the world today. Yet as with the trench coat, the origins of jeans are far removed from the world of fashion. This grandaddy of all blue jeans had its humble beginnings during the American Gold Rush at the end of the 19th century, when jeans were simply identified as 'waist overalls'. Originally manufactured from tent canvas, a tougher denim fabric was later substituted because the miners' complained about their poor durability.

In 1983 Yves Saint Laurent (1936–2008) confessed, 'I wish I had invented blue jeans. They have expression, modesty, sex appeal, simplicity – all I hope for in my clothes.' The reason the style has maintained its supremacy is because Levi's have been repeatedly mapped onto the evolution of one nation's culture and society. Their all-American image represents not only the nostalgia of an era of cowboys and Indians, but has also become the insignia of social revolution and glamour with ambassadors like Elvis Presley (1935–77), James Dean (1931–55) and latterly, President Barack Obama (b.1961), helping to perpetuate the mythology. Since their arrival as the staple of any fashion diet, denim jeans have been repeatedly adapted to fit into the silhouette of the prevailing trend, be it drain-piped, flared, cropped or oversized.

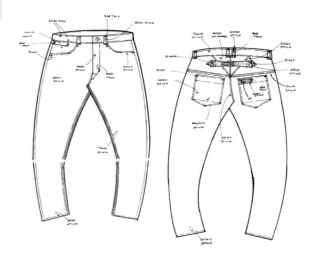

The little black dress

Coco Chanel was often quoted as saying 'Look for the woman in the dress. If there is no woman, there is no dress'. Her unique design philosophy revolutionized the 20th century dress code for women. She always advocated that the modern woman should dress plainly in dresses that were very simple in both shape and cut.

The original 'little black dress', or LBD for short, came into existence in 1926 and has continued to be selected as the must-have wardrobe component by most women. The LBD is the essence of chic, with its austere black lines accentuating the silhouette of the body. It truly never goes out of style no matter how many variations appear each season. The first LBD was a sleeveless sheath cut just above the knee that provided the wearer with an instantly effortlessly classic, stylish and sexy silhouette. At the time black was not considered an appropriate colour for fashionable clothes – it was a colour mainly set aside for funerals and mourning. Over time most fashion houses have produced their own version of the LBD and it has morphed into a fashion legend. The LBD's ultimate icon is Audrey Hepburn (1929–93), who famously wore a version of the LBD designed by Hubert de Givenchy (b.1927) as Holly Golightly in the film *Breakfast at Tiffany's* (1961).

Sketchbook task

3D-2D-3D

Pattern blocks are the traditional two-dimensional (2D) tools for developing shaping in pattern cutting. Used well, they offer a convenient shorthand approach to three-dimensional (3D) body fit. However, it is often beneficial to take a more lateral approach when building up new shapes and silhouettes. This is a simple exercise to free up your imagination and give you lots of unforeseen alternatives.

1. 3D–2D. Select an interesting 3-D object, not too large. Look for something that has an interesting shape rather than simply a cube or globe. It doesn't have to relate directly to fashion. Completely cover the object in layers of masking tape (you might want to protect the original beforehand by using cling film or similar). It doesn't matter if the tape overlaps – it will help strengthen the eventual pattern pieces. When you have blocked out the original with tape, mark out a series of cutting lines around the object. You can either follow the original's structure or invent your own. It is better to have smaller shapes rather than just a few blocked areas. It is also a good idea to add balance marks showing where one piece should join onto another, so that you can re-join the pieces once they are separated. Now carefully cut along your pattern lines to provide a series of flat pattern pieces for your 3D object. Then trace these out onto lightweight card or pattern paper and use a photocopier or scanner to enlarge the flat pattern shapes into various sizes. Make several duplicates of the enlarged pattern pieces. Finally, cut out the enlarged shapes.

2. 2D–3D. Once you have assembled your library of enlarged flat pattern shapes start by attaching them to a mannequin to generate new silhouettes around the body contours. Don't just work around the obvious areas of the dress form. Use your new pattern pieces to help you accentuate areas of the body that are usually neglected or enhance existing shapes by exaggerating their silhouette. Make interesting combinations of your pattern shapes either by adhering to the balance marks or using multiples of the same pattern piece.

3. Record your developments as you prepare your silhouettes either by photography or sketching and compile the results in your sketchbook.

'Reinvent new combinations of what you already own. Improvise. Become more creative. Not because you have to, but because you want to.'

Karl Lagerfeld (b.1933)

Conrad James Dawney (2012)
'My 3D object was one of my double-stacked Creepers. I thought it had a really interesting shape and would give me some great pattern pieces. It was really fun as I had never used this method of pattern cutting before, but I think I will be using it a lot in future, as the results I got from it were amazing. By moving things around, distorting the silhouette and thinking about new combinations, it gave me shapes that would have been difficult to create by just flat pattern cutting.'

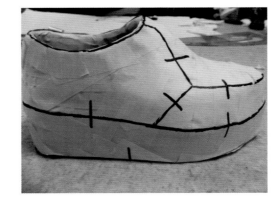 

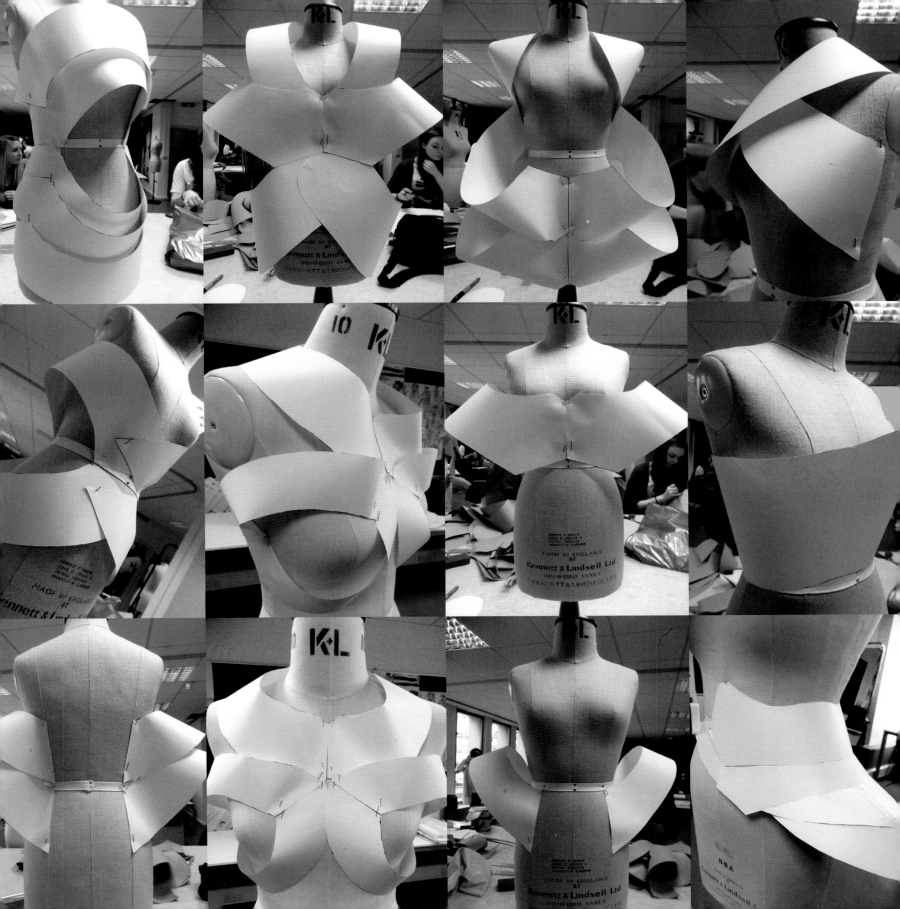

Sketchbook task

'Can you tell what it is, yet?'

Rolf Harris (b.1930)

Inkblots: what do YOU see?

Although the reliability of the outcomes of Hermann Rorschach's (1884–1922) inkblot test remain questionable by today's psychologists, the activity of staining and folding a piece of paper to create abstract patterns is a terrific way for any designer to test out their imagination. By exploiting the chance elements that result from inkblots, unpredictable things can happen that might not have presented themselves otherwise. Because of the mirroring effect, Rorschach inkblots can provide an excellent way to explore symmetry and investigate negative and positive spacing of images within the page.

Towards the end of his life, Andy Warhol famously made a series of 38 enormous pour-and-fold 'Rorschach' (1984) paintings by unrolling his canvas out on the studio floor, brushing a design on one side and then folding the canvas in half while the paint was still wet.

Orchestrating any inkblot towards a fashion conclusion is a spontaneous and creative way to develop both design ideas and illustrations. In the same way that the original test was used to reveal the unconscious workings of the mind by analyzing a patient's interpretation of the abstract shapes, for a fashion designer inkblots can help them to sidestep the logical and lock onto to their creative brain instead. Purposely ambiguous, these structureless inkblots will always be given a different purpose following each designer's actions.

You will need:
• Paper or lightweight card (heavy enough to hold wet media)
• Ink (preferably in a bottle with a dropper – or use a brush)
• Water (fill a recycled squeeze bottle).

To make a Rorschach inkblot:
1. Fold your paper/card in half and then apply a few squirts of water and a dot or two of ink to one half.
2. Fold over the blank half of the paper and apply pressure with the palm of your hand particularly at the folded edge.
3. Open out the paper and allow to dry.

You will also gain similarly rewarding results by expanding a single ink spillage with the addition of figurative lines to anchor the design on the page.

Left
Lotty Rose
(2012)
Gareth Pugh
Autumn/Winter
2012 Collection

<u>Right</u>
Danielle Meder (2009)
Gareth Pugh Autumn/Winter 2009 Collection.

<u>Above</u>
Joel Janse van Vuuren (2011)
'Chaos by Design'
'In developing my collection, I looked for
a method of design that was random and
would produce garments that were creative
from the outset. Rorschach's inkblots
sparked the idea of creating fashion
illustrations from inkblots. I placed the
paint on a page and either flattened another
page on top of it or folded the page in
half, both of which created interesting
silhouettes that could later be transformed
into fashion designs.'

Line and balance: establishing the visual equilibrium

Line in fashion design refers to the distinctive structural contour of the overall silhouette that is created by the cut and shaping of specific fabrics. It can also refer to the construction lines that divide up the space within the silhouetted outline. It remains one of the primary considerations when drawing or sketching out ideas because it is the fashion designer's most elementary means of putting ideas down on paper.

As well as resulting from shape and structure, the arrangement of decorative lines in fashion design can give the illusion of lengthening or shortening the figure in height, as well as making a body appear either larger or smaller. Because the eye tends to follow the line of a garment, a skilled designer can lure the gaze from one area of the body to another.

There can be any number of lines in fashion construction and design but most can be grouped as vertical, horizontal, diagonal, curved or radial.

In fashion design, balance can refer to the weighting within a collection or range of individual garments, so that the different components complement each other and work together as a total look.

'The dress must follow the body of a woman, not the body following the shape of the dress.'

Hubert de Givenchy

Left
Julie Campbell (2011)
The naturally balanced symmetry of the human figure is centered out from the spinal column and is mirror branched throughout the body's supporting bone structure.

zoom in detailing

Straight vertical lines will nearly always add height value and can make the body appear leaner and longer. The characteristic flapper silhouette from the 1920s was an example of vertical lines removing body curves at the waist and bust to suggest a slim, flattened, boyish figure.

Conversely, horizontal lines by and large, add weight and girth and can also reduce height; unsurprisingly most designers avoid using horizontal lines at the hips of the figure.

An asymmetrical diagonal line can be the most flattering as it snakes across the frame and suggests a softer, curvier effect than that obtained by severe vertical lines. Long diagonal lines falling across the body will also draw the eye downwards, accentuating both length and width. Diagonally cutting fabric, and working with the bias or cross-grain properties of the cloth found fame in the 1930s through the creations of Madeleine Vionnet (1876–1975), who earned herself the nickname of the 'Queen of the bias cut'.

A garment following curved lines will equally emphasize the curvature of the body and can provide a similar sensual appearance. A curved line imitates the organic lines of nature. A radial line is the designer's trap of drawing attention to a particular part of the figure. Used to create a neckline, radiating lines will always direct interest to the face.

<u>Above</u>
Amanda Brown (2012)

<u>Below</u>
Nicola Amodio (2012)
Increasing pattern construction lines in width or length can readjust the body's natural proportional values and accentuate the natural body dimensions to reflect the designer's concept.

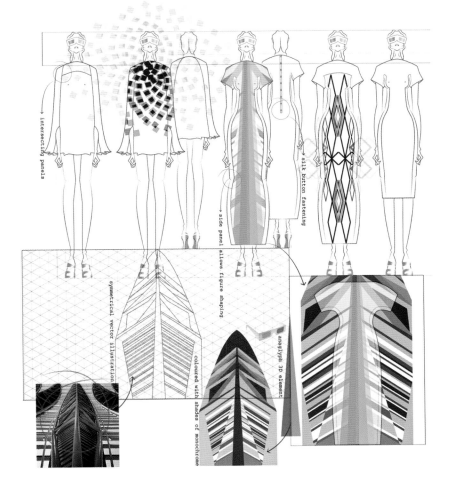

Here is a summary of some of the key fashion lines from the 19th and 20th centuries:

A-line created by Christian Dior (1905–57) in 1955 – suspended from the shoulders and extending over the hips and legs without a seamed waist – resembling a capital 'A'.

Chanel line established by Coco Chanel consisting of the boxy cardigan and straight or slightly flared skirt. Key elements of this style are the trimmings – buttons, braids and pearls.

'Corolle' and 'Huit' lines (dubbed 'The New Look' by Carmel Snow, editor of Harper's Bazaar) created in 1947 by Christian Dior – nipped-in waist, emphasized bust, wide calf-length skirt – worldwide impact following the Second World War.

Empire line popular throughout the Regency period, reminiscent of the classical Greek and Roman era with a high waist gathered beneath the bust and falling loosely to the feet – re-introduced in 1959 by Cristóbal Balenciaga (1895–1972) and widespread in traditional wedding gowns.

H-line created by Christian Dior in 1954–55 – a straight silhouette with a slender top and narrow hips, crossing at the hip – Dior also created the foundation garments that raised the bustline nearly 5cm (2in) and flattened the hipline.

Sack line launched by Hubert Givenchy in 1957 – straight waistless shift dress.

Trapèze line created by Yves Saint Laurent in 1958 – narrow shoulders flaring out like a pyramid towards the hem.

The Tulip line Dior 1953 collection – floaty, flower prints.

Twist line narrow-hipped outline with a slightly flared pleated skirt that flares as the wearer moves about.

Y-line designed by Dior in 1955–56 reversing his 'A' line look – placing the emphasis on the shoulders tapering down into narrow dresses or skirts to form the letter 'Y'.

I-line a narrow silhouette created by Cristóbal Balenciaga in 1954–55.

Pencil line created by Christian Dior in 1948 – tailored, figure-hugging skirt cut from the hips in one straight line down to the knee.

Princess line coat or dress cut in one without a waist seam – form-fitting shape achieved via vertical seams – credited to Charles Frederick Worth (1826–95) who made outfits for Empress Eugénie (1826–1920) of France in the mid-1800s.

S-line – appeared early 1900s – the result of wearing a straight-fronted corset finishing just below the bust that allowed the breasts to hang low and pressed the hips backwards to create a hollow-backed posture – Jacques Fath (1912–54) reintroduced the 'S'-line in 1954.

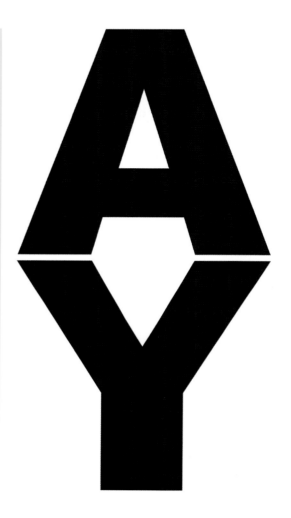

Key to the success of any fashion silhouette is the balance of the various sections inside the outlined frame. As with all accomplished design, balance for a fashion designer is the simple ordering of the parts of the whole, so that they work with each other, in order to provide a sense of visual equilibrium.

A designer relies upon seams, darts and cloth properties to manipulate their fabric to create the requisite lines and balance. Although prominent parts of the body (the hips, the bust, etc.) unsurprisingly require specific darting, draping or fabric suppression to follow the natural contours, these construction techniques are also employed all over the body to manipulate the fabric in order to provide new and provocative silhouettes. A tailor predominantly trusts to the tried-and-tested flat-pattern cutting techniques to mould the shape. Although most menswear will also be generated using these principles, the longer, uninterrupted lines offered by womenswear encourages designers to work directly onto a mannequin form, in unbleached calico, in order to sculpt the silhouette three-dimensionally.

Unlike the graphic designer who is primarily concerned with a 2-D output, the fashion designer's conclusion is ultimately viewed 'in the round', which means that balance is not just concerned with right and left or top and bottom, but also front and back. The fashion designer needs to consider every viewpoint and attempt to generate a sense of natural progression and continuity from one aspect to another.

In the 3D world of fashion, the rear and profile balance is an often-overlooked consideration. A wedding dress, for instance, is traditionally viewed as much from the back as from the front, and the contour silhouette of the Victorian bustle was only fully appreciated in side view.

Left
Beckie Docherty (2011)
The everyday lines in urban architecture can be easily transferred onto the fashion figure to articulate the sense of balance within a garment.

From an anatomical point of view, the measurement of the head is generally used to establish the proportions of the human body. In real life the average adult comprises approximately 7.5 heads in overall height. Although traditional dress stands are usually built to these proportions there is always a conflict between the real and ideal for the fashion designer when it comes to representing the body on paper. Despite the fact that their garments will ultimately have to fit a human body, it is characteristic in a fashion sketch to adopt a proportion balance more akin to 8.5 heads by stretching the lower body by the additional length. It has become a conventional practice by fashion designers and illustrators that seems more subconscious and intuitive than taught.

Opinions over body proportions have varied according to historical conventions and cultural differences. These are concerned not just with the cut of clothes to achieve a particular silhouette, but also with preferences for idealized body types. By tradition, all societies have their own ideas about what is considered beautiful.

Despite the more voluptuous figures of Marilyn Monroe (1926–62) and Brigitte Bardot (b.1934) during the 1950s, hourglass curves are no longer flaunted in the 2000s as the fashionable requisite for women. The ultra-thin female image that continues to appeal to contemporary fashion designers is a throwback to the same slender silhouette from the 1920s that has dominated the media's impression of fashion in film, centrefolds and press coverage during most of the 20th century.

The contemporary male fashion body (opposite) aspires more towards fitness and sports-derivative proportions with the 'V'-shaped torso of a broad chest, narrowing throughout the waist and hips, as the ultimate goal.

Within the Fine Arts, artists have always taken liberties and disregarded the body's natural proportions in order to represent their own interpretation of the ideal. In Ancient Greece, sculptor Polykleitos laid down his own strict rules about perfect proportion in the 5th century BC, by using eight heads high and two heads wide as the benchmark for representing the ideal male figure, and these proportional guidelines are still in use today at most life-drawing classes. Famously, Michelangelo's (1475–1564) revered marble statue of *David*, despite distorting both the size of the hands and head in proportion to the rest of the body, is universally recognized as the epitome of a beautifully proportioned body.

Allocating proportional differences within fashion design is also important to overall appearance and appeal. There are numerous demarcation lines available to the fashion designer when dividing up the silhouette, and these are determined by the cut and line of individual garments when brought together to create a total look or style. Generally speaking, the waistline is usually accepted as the obvious marker that the fashion designer uses in order to differentiate between the top and bottom of the figure, regardless of gender.

The natural pull of gravity has resulted in a common visual preference that expects more weight towards the bottom of a design. As a general rule, 3D objects appear more stable if the base looks proportionally heavier than the top. When the main distribution of weight is vertically higher, the overall composition or object can look precarious.

Using the waist as a demarcation point presents an uneven vertical proportion (2:3) that corresponds to the principles of the 'Golden Section' or 'Divine Proportion'. The Golden Section is a well-documented law of proportionality – a visual formula representing the symbol Φ (phi) that replicates the proportion and balance that occurs in space, physics, nature and mathematics. Because of this persistent reoccurrence throughout the known world, it has become accepted as a gauge of beauty and balance for most artists and designers. Its most famous figurative representation is probably in Leonardo Da Vinci's 1509 drawing, 'The Divine Proportion'.

The mathematical formula for the Golden Section is $\frac{1+\sqrt{5}}{2}$

'Project Runway' mentor, Tim Gunn (b.1953), has said 'Our perception of beauty, I believe, can be enhanced, but short of drinking some potion that hasn't yet been invented, I don't think that our perception of beauty can be totally and completely recalibrated. There are simply things that are more pleasing to the eye than others and we'll still want those things.'

Opposite, left
Eugene Czarneck
(2011)

Opposite, right
George Gozum (2012)

Right
Geoffry
Gertz (2010)

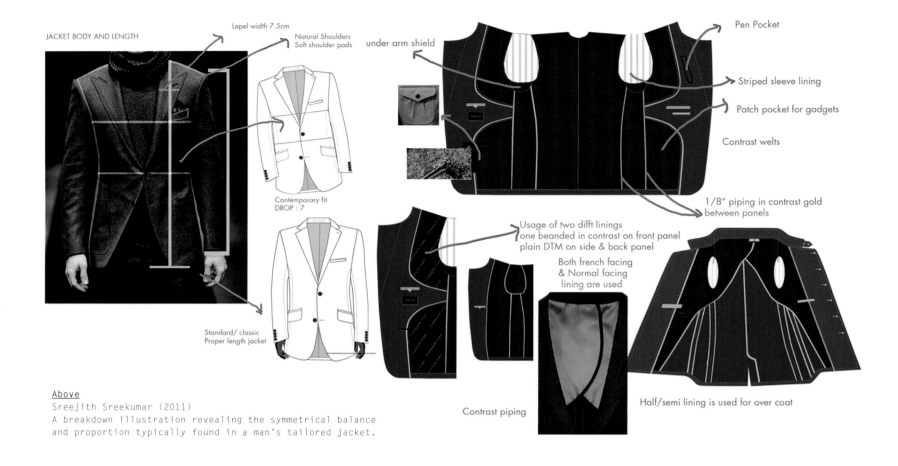

JACKET BODY AND LENGTH

Lapel width 7.5cm

Natural Shoulders
Soft shoulder pads

under arm shield

Pen Pocket

Striped sleeve lining

Patch pocket for gadgets

Contrast welts

Contemporary fit
DROP : 7

1/8" piping in contrast gold
between panels

Usage of two difft linings
one beanded in contrast on front panel
plain DTM on side & back panel

Both french facing
& Normal facing
lining are used

Standard/ classic
Proper length jacket

Contrast piping

Half/semi lining is used for over coat

<u>Above</u>
Sreejith Sreekumar (2011)
A breakdown illustration revealing the symmetrical balance
and proportion typically found in a man's tailored jacket.

There are two fundamental approaches to achieving balance within design: symmetrically or asymmetrically. Both values represent important concerns for every fashion designer attempting to dress the human body.

Symmetry is the norm for most of the man-made objects we encounter in daily life. Buildings, automobiles, tools and everyday utensils are all committed to a symmetrical balance. Because the human body is outwardly bilateral, with a mirror image either side of the central axis of the spine (two eyes, two ears, two arms, two legs, etc.), many designers automatically gravitate towards using a vertical symmetry. Identical balance will always guarantee equilibrium and harmony within the overall design. There will be minimal contrast or conflict between the parts and it stimulates a passive emotion. It provides the stability and permanence that is found in large architectural buildings, especially places of worship.

Consciously or unconsciously, a vertical symmetry is the familiar starting point when designing most fashion garments, because of the practicality of getting into and out of clothes. A central vertical opening on a blouse or coat is universally referred to as the 'centre front' or 'centre back' by pattern cutters, and it is conventional that trousers or jeans have a middle fastening point down from the waist. Buttoned or zipped, these design issues are as much about practical considerations as the aesthetics of the actual design. It should also not be overlooked that balance in fashion also works horizontally as well as vertically and top to bottom balance is equally as crucial.

However, an equal distribution throughout a design is often interpreted as playing safe – something that fashion is not known for. It is a more conservative view of balance; it can reduce the diversity of the output and become increasingly repetitive if a designer adheres too closely to this standardized template for balance. The traditional cut of a man's formal suit is a perfect example of mimicking the body's outward symmetry to create a prim and proper look.

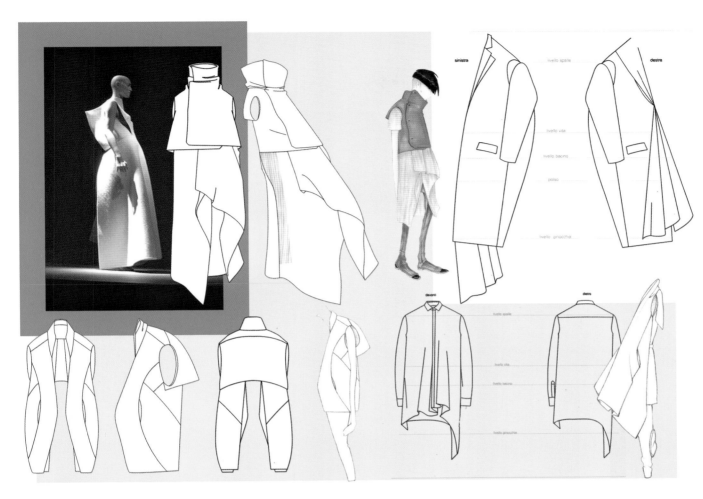

Left
Filomena Cavallaro
(2011)
Asymmetrical lines
are considered and
tested to achieve a
coherent balance to
the final garment's
shape and cut.

In fashion it is often considered more beneficial to throw off the balance in an attempt to achieve something regarded as 'out of the box'. The instant attraction of asymmetrical balance for any designer is the direct lack of a prescriptive formula or organization; it fuels the idea of freedom to take risks and experiment away from the norm.

At its most basic, asymmetry is regarded as the absence of symmetry. This deficiency of structured rules empowers designers to rely upon their own faculties of perception and it is ultimately down to an individual's personal sense of taste to recognize when the overall look is balanced as intended. As expected, with the safety net of a formula removed, it presents a greater challenge to the designer. The inherent instability of asymmetrical balance usually makes the results more dynamic and attention grabbing in appearance.

It is important to remember that the ultimate form of criticism in the world of fashion would be to be ignored. If a designer isn't featured in the media, it is tantamount to being classed unworthy of mention. Disturbing the balance of things creates that necessary catalyst. *Vogue* magazine's legendary editor-in-chief, Diana Vreeland (1903–89) said, 'Never fear being vulgar, just boring'. Contemporary fashion continues to tread the fine line between the agreeable and the disagreeable, the accepted and the unacceptable. Acclaimed designers such as Jean Paul Gaultier (b.1952), Alexander McQueen, Vivienne Westwood (b.1941) and Edward Meadham (b.1979)/Benjamin Kirchhoff (b.1978) – aka – Meadham Kirchhoff, owe a large amount of their fame to catwalk shock tactics that at one time or another have earned them the accolade of having 'questionable taste'.

The key consideration concerning silhouette, line and proportion for any fashion designer is that no matter how they are created or achieved; no matter which lines are used to differentiate the shape; no matter what balance between fabric, colour or pattern is employed, the end results must be both visually challenging and aesthetically balanced in form and structure. This balancing act is one of the most fundamental design problems facing any fashion designer and it is not unusual to generate page after page of alternative variations around a theme in order to hit upon the perfect balance.

Sketchbook task

'Without aesthetic, design is either the humdrum repetition of familiar clichés or a wild scramble for novelty.'

Paul Rand (1914-96)

Reflecting on symmetry

The symmetry and balance of the body is often difficult to block out when you begin to design garments. The vertical axis of the skeleton, and the balance of its left and right distribution, is a subconscious template trap that can inhibit you from experimenting away from the equilibrium of the human physique. This exercise will make you investigate an alternative linear balance that doesn't reply upon human symmetry for its aesthetic appeal. By transferring lines that appear in the environment into your sketchbook you will be able to assemble unconventional skeletons that provide an alternative basis for your eventual garment designs.

1. You need to equip yourself with a camera before setting out to track down evidence of man-made lines that have been 'drawn' within your immediate urban surroundings. You will not need to stray very far – lines can be seen everywhere in every city environment: road markings, train tracks, scaffolding, wrought, iron gates, etc. You should aim to locate a mix of both curved and straight lines. Lines that cross one another will also provide you with boundaries. Photographically, frame the lines from a variety of unusual angles to assemble a library of interesting linear patterns. The task works best if there is a strong contrast between the lines and their background so that they are easier to pick out.

2. When you return home, print out multiples of your photographs as large as possible. You might want to drain away the colour or boost the contrast so that you are left with bold monochromatic lines. Now, cut out a series of chance shapes from your photographs by following the lines within your photographs. Group these shapes together to generate figurative outlines. Try to reduce the normal vertical and horizontal skeleton by using curved, diagonal, twisted or zigzag alternatives. Exploit both the scale and rhythm of the lines but always make sure that there is a continuous flow of lines throughout the composition to bind everything together. Remember that a line is often described as an elongated dot. Artist Paul Klee (1879–1940) famously added that 'a line is a dot that went for a walk'.

3. Transfer the results into your sketchbook.

Below and right
Kayleigh Macbeth (2011)
'Glasgow Palm House'
'The Botanic Gardens lies
in the West End of Glasgow
and is famous for its glass
houses. The Kibble Palace
is my favourite of the two
because of its Art Nouveau
curves and shapes. The
structure offered me such
beautiful lines and shapes.
As a fashion designer I
am always thinking how
these qualities could
transform into garments.
I cut up sections of the
photographs and composed
them in a state in which
I §could envision new
figurative silhouettes.'

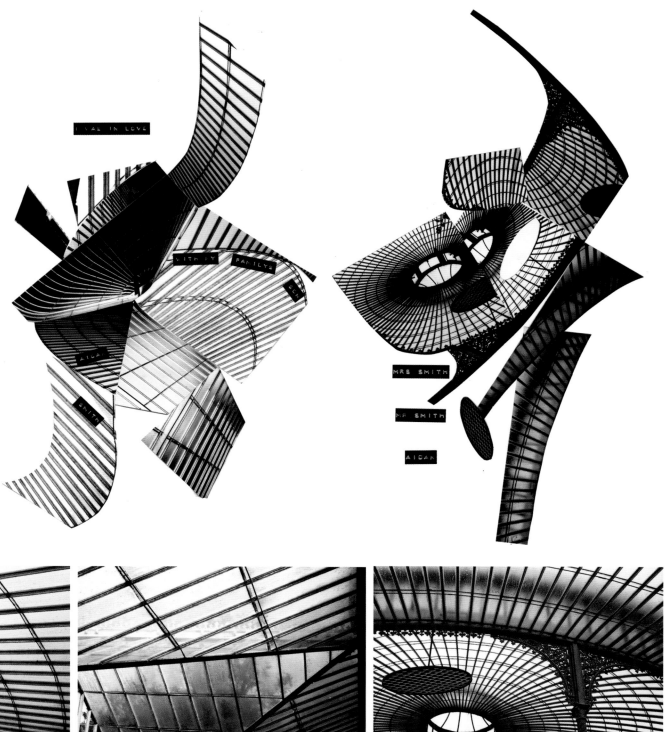

Sketchbook task

'Today's clothing is the workman's overall.'

Varvara Stepanova (1894–1958)

Keep it simple: 60-second Constructivist fashion

Husband and wife, Alexander Rodchenko (1891–1956) and Varvara Stepanova, were part of the cultural overhaul that both pre-dated and followed the Russian Revolution of 1917, and set in motion the Constructivist artistic movement that impacted on the visual arts in Russia. The principle that art should be readily available to the ordinary working man and woman was the premise that drove their beliefs and resulted in a unique expressive style that employed simple geometric shapes, bold blocks of colour and usually incorporated dramatic fonts. Their eye-catching style remains a muse for designers today and in 2005 famously became the inspiration for Franz Ferdinand's 'You Could Have It So Much Better' album cover. The Scottish band had already adapted Constructivist El Lissitzky's (1890–1941) 1919 Soviet propaganda poster, 'Beat the Whites with the Red Wedge' for their fifth single artwork, 'This Fffire'.

This is a challenging but rewarding task that restricts you to using simple geometric outlines rather than conventional pattern blocks to test out non-traditional methods of achieving garment structures and silhouettes.

1. Prepare a series of different-sized squares, triangles and circles in card or heavyweight paper. Try experimenting with a different colour for each geometric shape.

2. Using a dress stand, attach the shapes to create geometric patterns across the form without necessarily adhering to the established construction of garments that require centre openings or armholes, etc. Instead, place the shapes where you feel that they present an interesting and balanced layout across the mannequin. It helps if you give yourself a time limit per geometric arrangement – a 60-second window will keep your ideas impulsive and spontaneous.

3. Document your new shapes as you achieve them and arrange them with contextual back-up reference in your sketchbook.

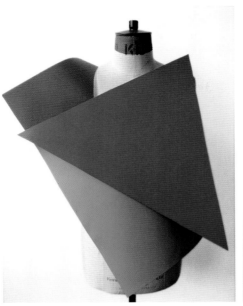
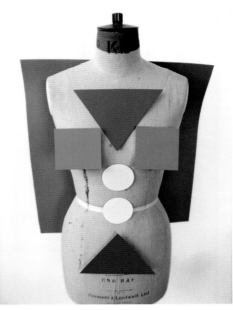
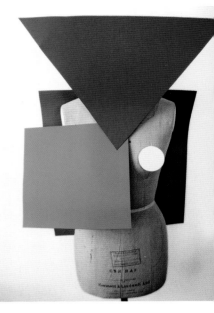

<u>Opposite</u>
El Lizzitzky (1919)
'Beat the Whites with the
Red Wedge'

<u>This page</u>
Samme Williams (2011)

Shape, form and texture: the fabric of fashion

An inherent problem for the fashion designer working with a sketchbook is that, in construction, the design work will move from the 2D page to a 3D shape.

A sketchbook page can never replace the tactile awareness of handling fabric and physically fashioning a garment at a full 360º on a dress stand. But that is not its purpose. As has already been outlined, a fashion sketchbook is the place to house all manner of potential stimulus for future design and to support its eventual transition from paper to 3D form. Most designers use their sketchbooks as their personal sounding board for ideas before physically putting them into practice. At times ideas that work well on paper don't materialize as successfully in reality. This is often explained by the relaxed nature and privacy of the sketchbook as opposed to the spotlight exposure of working in the round. However, a fashion designer needs to bridge this divide and feel as confident in 3D as they are in 2D.

Ultimately, the building blocks for any designer are the materials used to fully realize the design ideas. For the fashion designer, fabric always sits at the heart of the creative practice. Fabric choice is crucial and is judged to be a make-or-break decision. Selecting the correct fabric is vital because it acts as the medium that anchors the colour and sculpts the silhouette of the garment. It needs careful consideration on several levels because all fabric structures have their own inherent properties that can be used to assist in the construction of volume and shape.

Below left
Hâf Evans (2012)

Below right
Rosa Ng (2011)
As well as archiving fabric sources your fashion sketchbook needs to act as a repository for shape experiments using 3-D texture.

Neoprene & laser cutting sampling

Above
Tiffany Baron (2012)
Technology has
widened the fabric
library for the
fashion designer and
impacted upon the
tools that are used
to achieve shape and
texture.

Stretch fabrics like Lycra and jersey will cling to the body and enhance a natural contour, whereas stiffer and less elastic fabrics like a duck canvas or linen, are capable of sculpting and holding a stronger outline away from the figure. The texture of a given fabric will also influence how the colour will appear. A fine, transparent material like chiffon or organdie will mute the palette while shiny PVC and plastic surfaces will reflect and add a harsh gloss.

The texture of a fabric will also impact on how the design lines function within a garment. By using the cross-grain of a woven cloth rather than following the straight grain of the selvage, bias draping can be achieved, while the hard-wearing cotton twill of a denim has a stability to support and benefit from multiple lines of top-stitching. The weight of a cloth will also dictate the way a garment hangs or falls away from the body. A coarse tweed or loden cloth will remain firm and solid, whereas a lace fabric will collapse in volume without adequate support.

In addition to employing the inherent natural properties of any cloth, most fabrics can also be manipulated to facilitate the creation of a desired form. Fabric can be sculpted in various ways to build up a required shape (darting, draping, pleating, etc.) and structures can be put in place to underpin the shaping (padding, canvas, boning, etc.). Fabric also lends itself to being embellished with surface pattern or decoration to enhance the shape and form as well as intensifying the aesthetic qualities of the garment.

Over time, technological advances have continued to augment the traditional fabric library. Nylon, first registered by DuPont in 1939 as 'a miracle fiber for women's stockings' paved the way for other synthetic fibres such as Orlon, Dacron and Polyester. Contemporary sportswear has benefited more than any other type of garment from the developments of performance-driven fabrics. Labels, such a Nike, Inc. have exploited these improvements to establish their own individual style and appeal. Triumph launched their solar-powered swimwear in 2008, sporting front panels to harness enough power to charge an iPod or mobile phone and Ermenegildo Zegna (1892–1966) used the same smart technology embedded into the neoprene collars of his sk-jacket range.

Popular fashion fabrics

Here is a quick summary of some of the most popular fashion yarns and fabrics available to the fashion designer:

Brocade
A rich, heavy jacquard weave set against a satin weave background and named after the Italian 'broccato' meaning 'embossed cloth'.

Calico
A coarse, undyed plain-weave cotton with a smooth surface that originated in Calicut, India and is usually sized for crispness.

Canvas/duck
A durable, closely woven, even fabric that is both heavy and strong.

Cashmere
A luxury soft fibre combed from the undercoat of the Kashmir mountain goats from Mongolia and the Himalayas.

Cheesecloth
Originally a wrapping for cheese, this is a loosely woven, plain-weave fabric with an open construction.

Chenille
A tufty, soft-pile yarn cut into strips as a trimming and named after the French for 'hairy caterpillar'.

Crêpe
A lightweight fabric characterized by its crinkly, crimped, grained textured surface and named after the French *cespe* meaning 'curled'.

Crêpe de Chine
A sheer, delicate fabric with a rippled surface made by mixing silk with synthetic threads.

Chiffon
A very delicate, diaphanous fine crêpe fabric with an open weave using twisted yarns.

Corduroy
A cut-pile fabric with a variety of different rib ('wales') widths and depths with a soft, velvet-like nap.

Cotton
A classic fabric obtained from vegetable fibre available in a variety of types depending on the plant (Egyptian cotton, Sea Island Cotton, American Upland Cotton and Asiatic Cotton).

Denim
A hard-wearing cotton twill weave with a distinctive indigo warp and a white weft that resists snagging and tears.

Flannel
A durable woollen/cotton weave with a strong yet soft texture.

Gabardine
A naturally waterproof, durable, tightly woven, steep-twilled fabric with a distinctive diagonal twill rib.

Georgette
A sheer, lightweight plain weave fabric, similar to chiffon, that has a crisp texture and dull surface, named after 19th-century French dressmaker, Georgette de la Plante.

Gauze
A thin, translucent fabric, with a loose open weave.

Gingham
A light, plain-weave cotton made from alternating white and coloured threads to create a gingham 'stripe' or 'check'.

Jersey
A very elastic, single-knit fabric from plain and purl stitches with special crease-resistant properties first produced as fisherman's sweaters on the island of Jersey.

Lace
A decorative, openwork fabric constructed from a network of fine threads.

Lamé
A luxurious brocade using a warp of interwoven metallic threads giving it a glittery surface. The name comes from the French for 'worked with gold and silver wire'.

Lawn
A lightweight, fine, plain-weave cotton or linen with a crisp finish. The term is derived from Laon, a French city important in the manufacture of linen.

Linen
One of the oldest textiles in the world that uses vegetable fibre from the flax plant.

Lycra
A light fabric constructed from a polyurethane fibre with lots of elasticity.

Melton
A very solid woven wool with a clipped brushed nap similar to felt; originated in Melton, England.

Mohair
Yarn made from the lustrous, wiry hair of the Angora goat.

Moiré
A distinctive rippling pattern with characteristic wave reflections due to its contrasting crushed and uncrushed weave.

Muslin
A semi-transparent, plain-weave fabric, originally made from silk or cotton, but now made from almost anything.

Nylon
A water-resistant, man-made fibre with superb elasticity, almost impervious to abrasion.

Organdie
A fine, translucent plain-weave cotton similar to muslin.

Organza
A stiff, plain-weave fabric resembling organdie but made from silk or synthetic threads.

Poplin
A mercerized, plain-weave cotton with a corded surface, caused by the warp threads doubling the number of weft threads.

PVC
The abbreviated name for Polyvinyl chloride, a very hard-wearing, waterproof synthetic fabric derived from petrochemicals; first patented in 1913.

Sateen
A strong cotton fabric with a satin-weave giving a smooth sheen to the surface.

Satin
A smooth fabric with a distinctive lustrous and glossy surface caused by its floating warp; originating in Zaytoun (now Canton), China.

Seersucker
A dull-surfaced cotton fabric featuring flat and puckered striped sections.

Shantung
Originally a fine, hand-loomed raw silk with an irregular surface caused by the slubbed yarns; originating in the Chinese province of Shantung.

Silk
A luxury fabric made from the natural fibre produced by the silkworm – a tradition originally only known by the Chinese.

Taffeta
A rustling, closely woven, plain-weave fabric with a crisp feel – derived from the Persian *taftah* meaning 'silken cloth'.

Tulle
A sheer and delicate lightweight silk netting, often starched, commonly used in wedding veils and ballet tutus.

Tweed
A thick, homespun fabric with a rough surface and distinctively patterned or speckled in appearance; originally produced on the banks of the River Tweed in Scotland.

Velour
A thick, short, plush pile knitted or woven fabric with a pile of uneven lengths; *velours* is the French for 'velvet'.

Velvet
A soft fabric with a dense, closely cut hairy pile nap constructed from an extra warp yarn; from the Latin for 'hairy'.

Viyella
The registered trademark for a fine, brushed wool or cotton-blended fabric with a twill weave.

Voile
A very lightweight, semi-transparent cloth made from highly twisted yarns with a hard finish.

Wool
A natural fibre obtained from the fleece of sheep, llamas and goats that produces a dull-surfaced fabric celebrated for its warmth.

Sketchbook task

'The Souper Dress/No Cleaning/No Washing/It's carefree
fire resistant unless washed or cleaned/To refreshen,
press lightly with warm iron'.

Label in paper Souper Dress, after Warhol,
by Campbell's Soup Company (1968)

Ready-to-tear: paper fashion

Paper may not be the first medium you might think of when you imagine building a 3D structure, but for a fashion designer it has qualities that lend themselves to the testing out of new shapes and forms. The same piece of paper can become rigid and stiff (when pleated) and flexible and fluid (when slit). Unlike woven cloth, it does not naturally fray, unless you do it yourself, and its surface can also be instantly transformed by adding colour or heat. Mistakes are easily remedied by an adhesive tape or glue repair and if necessary, the entire process can be started all over again, because paper is still a very cost-effective material to use. Whether you are working with patchwork post-it notes or a roll of wallpaper, the medium offers the fashion designer untold benefits for experimentation.

During the mid-1960s disposable paper clothes became a short-lived fashion phenomenon in America following a marketing stunt by the inventors of the paper towel. Purchasers of their A-line 'Paper Caper' dresses, available in two striking gift-wrap designs, also received discount coupons for their other paper products. Within six months the company had received requests for over half a million dresses. The shift dresses were made from their paper-napkin stock reinforced with rayon webbing that they branded as DuraWeave.

More recently Hussein Chalayan (b.1970) created an 'Airmail Dress' from a standard blue aerogram for his 1998 collection, while Issey Miyake (b.1938) sculpted dresses from the recycled pleated rice paper that he employs to create his intricate 'Pleats Please' collections.

1. Using paper as your medium, invent a series of experimental garment shapes and textures. As well as treating the paper as you would any other fabric, adapt your working methods to match the properties of the paper stock. Test out the same techniques with differing weights of paper, the results may surprise you.

2. Capture the results in your sketchbook.

Sketchbook task

'Constant repetition carries conviction.'

Robert Collier (1885-1950)

Multiple fashion

Francisco Rabaneda Cuervo (b.1934), commonly known as Paco Rabanne, became notorious during the 1960s for his futuristic garments made from plastic and metal. Using techniques borrowed from jewellery, they were constructed from simple, repeated, interlinked shapes that imitated medieval chain mail. Needle and thread had been abandoned in favour of wire and pliers in order to bring the garments into being. His success was immediate even though some of the dresses weighed over 27kg (60lb). By 1966, Rabanne had opened his own boutique in Paris selling his ready-to-wear plastic dresses, and even supplying some in kit form for the more adventurous. His first collection was publicized as '12 Unwearable Dresses in Contemporary Materials' with the garments shaped directly onto a living body rather than through conventional pattern cutting. Coco Chanel famously referred to Rabanne as 'the metalworker of fashion'. His signature style later crossed into popular culture when worn by Audrey Hepburn in 'Two for the Road' (1967) and Jane Fonda (b.1937) as 'Barbarella' (1968).

Although he formally retired in 1999, Rabanne's legacy has inspired contemporary fashion designers such as Yohji Yamamoto (b.1943) and Helmut Lang (b.1956). In the UK, the Selfridges department store in Birmingham is covered with over 15,000 shiny aluminum disks, and is very obviously inspired by Rabanne's chain-mail dresses.

The repetition of a single basic unit works well in garment design. Here is an uncomplicated task to add interest to your designs by the duplication of a single item to create a fabric, trim or accessory in the style of Paco Rabanne.

1. Locate a readily available 3D object that you can multiply in quantity. You will need to join these together – so its fabrication might be a consideration (or a challenge!).

2. Begin by combining several of the units together to see what type of structure they make. Play with this across the body to find out where it appears best suited.

3. Once you are happy with its placement on the body, continue to manufacture your fabric, trim or accessory by adding more and more units together to build up your shape.

4. Document your progress from a single unit through to the finished article and add to your fashion sketchbook.

Below
Outi Pyy (2009)
'Zip Teeth Belt'
(Photography OutsaPop Trashion.)

Showcase 1

Name
Jade Elizabeth Hannam
Nationality
British
Graduate
Bradford College, UK
Collection 2010-11
'Wheels of Heritage'

'My sketchbook is the theory behind the practical; it is the bones for any project and I would never design without one. I consider myself to be a very visual person – anything and everything inspires me. Sometimes inspiration strikes from the most unusual places; it's uncontrollable! A lot of my ideas stem from my personal surroundings and experiences. Whenever I start a new project I always start with the question, 'What does this mean to me?' To answer this I search through books, photographs, and objects, go to galleries and museums, anywhere that might prove influential. If I were to label my method, I would say I am an 'inspiration hoarder!'

I keep a general sketchbook for anything that I find interesting; you never know what might spark a new concept and ideas are easily forgotten if you don't record them. Because I like to use a lot of print in my designs, I often create a separate sketchbook of research that can be developed into print designs. I am picky about my sketchbooks; I like A4, good thick paper, black cover and book bound.

When I have collated all my ideas I develop them through sketching and photography. I use a lot of different media because this often leads to fabric and print ideas. I start with my primary research, mood, inspiration and colour boards, my 'findings' so to speak. Then I develop my ideas for a colour palette and design details by researching into trends, colour prediction and market research. I also start to moulage fabric onto the mannequin, creating freehand shapes and silhouettes. I photograph these and sketch over them to further develop my concept.

My 'Wheels of Heritage' project was based around my own family history in Bradford. During the years of 1896–98 my many times 'great' grandad was the Lord Mayor of Bradford – that is when Bradford became a city and was still regarded as a hub of the woollen industry. I garnered my ideas by visiting all the old buildings in Bradford that were associated with my family. I sketched portions of the Town Hall, old mills and all the wool, combing machines in the textile museum, re-working all the details into garment and print ideas in my sketchbooks.

I consider my sketchbook to be the heart of my project; everything starts there before stemming out into the final outcome. My sketchbook allows me to explore what works and what doesn't. It allows me to document my tests and trials, which is crucial in all design. A sketchbook provides the opportunity to explore your artistic language, it helps you solve problems and permits you to reflect on your personal development.'

CHAPTER 2

Investigation: where to find your reference?

'Nothing is original. Steal from anywhere that resonates with inspiration or fuels your imagination. Devour old films, new films, music, books, paintings, photographs, poems, dreams, random conversations, architecture, bridges, street signs, trees, clouds, bodies of water, light and shadows. Select only things to steal from that speak directly to your soul. If you do this, your work (and theft) will be authentic. Authenticity is invaluable; originality is non-existent. And don't bother concealing your thievery – celebrate it if you feel like it. In any case, always remember what Jean-Luc Godard said: 'It's not where you take things from – it's where you take them to.'

Jim Jarmusch (b.1953)

Now that you know what is needed for a successful sketchbook, you should learn where to look in order to obtain your inspiration and ideas. There is a wealth of easily accessible visual reference to stimulate your creative imagination once you know where to find it. It is already out there, ripe for the picking, and you just need to capture it in your sketchbook.

This chapter will identify key areas that are always useful resources for the fashion designer. There are two basic methods of obtaining your research: primary and secondary. Primary research is conducted first hand, usually by drawing or photography. It is sourced and recorded by each individual designer and is therefore personal and subjective in its selection. With primary research there is also the potential to enrich the documentation with tactile artefacts collected along the way. These provide the distinctive 'touchy-feely' element that is prevalent in the majority of fashion designers' sketchbooks.

Secondary research is the work of others that you have identified and want to catalogue for reference purposes, and is the best method for documenting things that are no longer available to view at first hand or not easily accessible (i.e. events, historical data, private collections, etc.). Neither one is better than the other – they both form part of a designer's research journey. Although at the click of a mouse, a high-definition webcam can instantly open a window on a foreign country and climate, it can only report the cold facts. Always remember that the taste, smell and ambiance of a physical environment can never be totally conveyed via the sterile screen of a computer's monitor.

A good designer will inevitably resort to using both methods when trawling for ideas, feelings and inspirational information.

As well as directing your investigation towards fashion in a literal way, it is also necessary to look away from fashion so that you can bring something new and fresh into the designer mix. Hussein Chalayan said 'The more experience you have outside of fashion, the more enriched you will be.'

Above
Les Puces, Paris
(Photography © Julien Foucher.)

Opposite
Camden Town, London
(Photography © Conrad James Dawney.)
Always rewarding to the fashion researcher, are the vintage and second-hand market stalls that proliferate
in most capital cities around the world. By necessity they require an element of exploration to unearth their
treasures. Filling 7 hectares, the largest and most famous flea market is the one at Porte de Clignancourt in
Paris, officially called Les Puces de Saint-Ouen, but known the world over as Les Puces ('The Fleas').

Primary sources

'Wish you were here!': cultural awareness

> 'When I discovered Marrakech, it was an extraordinary shock.
> The city taught me color.'

Yves Saint Laurent

All artists and designers can bring fresh insights and forms to their work by the exploration and discovery of alternative traditions. Pablo Picasso (1881–1973) famously drew inspiration from African masks, and Tahitian culture had a life-changing effect upon the paintings of Paul Gauguin (1848–1903).

A cultural visit is one of the most enjoyable and rewarding means of personally experiencing and stockpiling a wealth of valuable inspiration for future reference. The current accessibility of low-cost travel has given everyone the opportunity to gain first-hand knowledge of other cultures and lifestyles. Most schools and colleges have taken advantage of affordable travel and now include cultural visits abroad within their curriculum. Designers often travel around the world as part of their compulsory attendance at international trade fairs and symposiums. As well as the obvious visual delights of different lifestyles, represented by national costume or regional architecture, there are also the non-tangible aspects of the surroundings that a different culture can offer to a designer.

Being on the spot and soaking up the local colour is a matchless experience that commands documentation in your sketchbook: the food, travel, geography, and nightlife are features that tour operators are always keen to highlight as special to a particular area. But these aspects are also valuable factors that a designer can draw upon and should record instinctively.

Above and right
Celebrations as diverse as New York's annual Easter Bonnet Parade (photography © Geoffry Gertz) or a religious ceremony in Vietnam's Cao Dai Temple (photography © Liliana Rodriguez) offer unlimited research potential for the culture-hungry traveller.

Opposite
Kayleigh Jean Allen (2011)
A trip to Berlin generated varied visual plunder for the sketchbook.

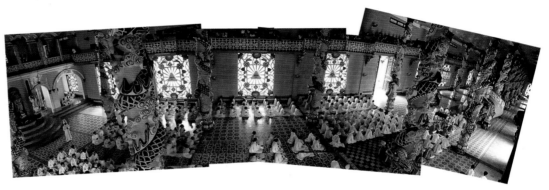

Observing a street festival as part of Chinese New Year, or watching a carnival parade in Rio de Janeiro or London's Notting Hill Gate, adds up to more than just a visual extravaganza. It is also about imbuing oneself with the atmosphere of a cultural legacy – the intangible sounds and smells, and the emotional kick that stimulates the senses. In a similar way, the choreographic etiquette and serenity of the traditional Japanese Tea Ceremony (*Ocha*) or the infectious and pulsating *Fiestas patronales* held across Latin America and Spain, are best appreciated first hand and captured using a variety of primary research memorabilia.

At the time these experiences might not seem immediately transferable, but the opportunity of coming face-to-face with cultural differences and experiencing foreign locations should never be written off as simply an excuse for a holiday snap. As well as drawing or using a camera to capture and chronicle your encounters, collecting the ephemera of a journey, such as travel tickets and maps, food wrappers and labels, local newspapers and currency, postage stamps and vintage postcards can breathe life into the experience during any future examination of your findings.

'The more isolated you are from the rest of the world, the more curious you are, the more you want to discover. I have always been an innately curious person, fueling this even further.'

Hussein Chalayan

Left
Olga Vokalova (2011)
An excursion to Paris is captured in the sketchbook for future design development.

Right
Hannah Dowds (2009)
Using a sketchbook as a repository for the weird and wonderful. The abstract expressionist painter Hans Hoffman (1880-1966) said 'The whole world, as we experience it visually, comes to us through the mystic realm of colour.'

TEN POPULAR CITY DESTINATIONS AROUND THE WORLD WITH LANDMARK BUILDINGS
Seattle, USA Landmark: Space Needle
San Francisco, USA Landmark: Golden Gate Bridge
New York, USA Landmark: Empire State Building
Paris, France Landmark: Eiffel Tower
Barcelona, Spain Landmark: La Sagrada Família
London, UK Landmark: Trafalgar Square
Rome, Italy Landmark: Colosseum
Florence, Italy Landmark: Basilica di Santa Maria del Fiore
Venice, Italy Landmark: Piazza San Marco
Sydney, Australia Landmark: Sydney Opera House

Learning to look: observational drawing

Drawing is the most instant and accessible method of obtaining primary research. Observing and capturing visual stimuli through drawing is within every designer's grasp. Although everybody draws differently, most designers begin their research with detailed observational drawings executed from primary research. By focusing the attention, the drawing process forces the designer to look carefully at the subject and increases both perception and observational skills. It provides the opportunity to simplify the complexities of the visual world.

'Until we can insert a USB into our ear and download our thoughts, drawing remains the best way of getting visual information on to the page.'

Grayson Perry
(b. 1960)

Observational drawing is all about capturing the reality of life – its people, objects and environments. There is little point in reiterating 2D images – they are already flat.

The fashion designer can undoubtedly nurture new ideas through observational drawing since it operates as a spontaneous feeder and conduit. At its best, observational drawing should be a true recording of what is witnessed without altering the subject, although it will obviously necessitate a personal response and an element of interpretation.

Annotating the drawings by the inclusion of scribbled comments is equally worthwhile. Shorthand notes not only catalogue the drawing through the factual data of dates and location, but also provide an opportunity for the designer to write down emotional feelings and experiences at that time.

Drawing a figure from life is the time-honoured cornerstone of traditional art training and is regarded as a disciplined art form in its own right. Most artists still maintain that this remains the truest and most authentic method of learning how to capture the 3-D shape and contours of the human body.

Opposite
Geoffry
Gertz (2011)

Left
Meagan
Morrison
(2010)

The majority of art schools still maintain the practice of drawing a naked figure as part of their curriculum. For fashion designers or illustrators, life-drawing classes offer a perfect opportunity to familiarize themselves with the basic anatomy of the human body in terms of posture and proportion. However, it is equally important to capture the clothed figure. As a fashion designer, observational drawing showing a fabric's texture or how a cloth drapes across a body, supplies an indispensable 2D awareness.

Costume life drawing is a given for any fashion designer carrying out research since it allows close scrutiny of all three aspects needed for the research and future illustration of fashion: colour, silhouette and texture. Close observational drawing can reveal the fundamental composition and structure of garments.

Continued observational drawing will build up the necessary confidence with which other types of drawing can then be undertaken; it is the starting point for any future illustrative styles and approaches.

'I was literally three years old when I started drawing. I did it all my life, through primary school, secondary school, all my life. I always, always wanted to be a designer. I read books on fashion from the age of 12. I followed designer's careers. I knew Giorgio Armani was a window-dresser, Emanuel Ungaro was a tailor.'

Alexander McQueen

Opposite
Designers, illustrators and artists sketching from a fashion model at the monthly NYC Model Meet-Up at The Centre in the West Village.
(Photography © Christopher Musci.)

Left
Clifford Faust (2011)

TEN INFLUENTIAL FIGURATIVE ARTISTS AND PAINTERS

Count Balthasar Klossowski de Rola (Balthus) (Polish/French artist 1908-2001)
Kenyon Cox (American painter 1856-1919)
Edgar Degas (French artist 1834-1917)
Lucian Freud (British painter 1922-2011)
Tamara de Lempicka (Polish painter 1898-1980)
Leonardo di ser Piero da Vinci (Italian artist 1452-1519)
Édouard Manet (French painter 1832-83)
Michelangelo di Lodovico Buonarroti Simoni (Italian artist 1475-1564)
Ilya Yefimovich Repin (Russian/Ukrainian artist 1844-1930)
Egon Schiele (Austrian painter 1890-1918)

Looking beyond the past: museums

Today, more than ever, artists and designers require a familiarity with the past to understand the references of contemporary art and practice, and the museum is the natural stopping-off point for research by all savvy fashion designers. Whether following a specific quest or just as a casual browser, museums and galleries continue to reward any inquisitive designer undertaking primary research. They provide an Aladdin's cave of wonderment and visual delight that at times can appear overwhelming due to the immense scale of their collected works.

The vast resources of the Victoria and Albert Museum in London, the Louvre Museum in Paris or the Metropolitan Museum in New York make them daunting institutions of incomparable cultural and historical importance. Their collections are truly staggering and will always be irresistible for any design related investigation; the only dilemma facing each researcher is how to decipher the multitude of available visual material.

Right
Beauty in Black at the National Museum of Singapore in 2011 explored the iconic status of the colour black in contemporary fashion and its continual appeal to both the wearer and fashion designers. Dresses from the 1950s to 2000s by leading fashion designers from the West including Cristóbal Balenciaga, Pierre Cardin (b.1922), Karl Lagerfeld and Azzedine Alaïa (b.1939), were exhibited alongside garments that were made and designed locally in Singapore including pieces by Benny Ong (b.1949) and Thomas Wee.
(Photography courtesy National Museum of Singapore.)

For more specialist study there are also fashion museums around the world that supply a more focused appraisal. The Musée de la Mode et du Textile in Paris houses the world's largest collection of costume and fashion, but it will only ever be possible to view it in its entirety via their frequently changing exhibitions. The Museum at the Fashion Institute of Technology (MFIT) is the only museum in New York City dedicated solely to the art of fashion. The museum has a collection of more than 50,000 garments and accessories dating from the 18th century to the present. Like other fashion museums, such as the Musée de la Mode, the ModeMuseum (MoMu) in Antwerp, Belgium and the Museo de la Moda in Santiago, Chile, The Museum at FIT collects, conserves, documents, and exhibits for future researchers.

'I came to realise early on that I would discover something new by exploring the stunning achievements of people before me. Thus I have been recognized as an innovator.'

Vivienne Westwood

There are increasingly regular thematic displays devoted to a single fashion theme or designer held at MoMu. The Fashion Museum in Bath, England is a smaller institution, but no less equally rewarding in its assembled display cases of historic costume. Some museums are dedicated to showcasing just single items of clothing, as with The Fan Museum in Greenwich, London or the Knopf und Knopf International Museum of Buttons in Warthausen, Germany. Whatever their size or specialism, all museums have the potential to provide designers with first-hand opportunities to appreciate how designers worked in the past. They are places where a garment or outfit can be contemplated and where the form, material, cut, processing and concept of fashion design can be enjoyed.

Right
Behind the Scenes at the Fashion Museum (2011) provided the opportunity for visitors to Bath to see a series of chronological display installations showcasing historic fashions from the museum collection. Manager of the Fashion Museum, Rosemary Harden said: 'We are giving visitors a glimpse through the keyhole, and inviting them behind the scenes into the museum store. The collection here at the Council's Fashion Museum is so numerous and so full of treasures, this is a great new way to share the collection and to convey that sense of wonder to our visitors. We're describing it as a sort of *Narnia* experience, stepping into the biggest wardrobe ever, with at least 100 years worth of clothes.'
(Photography courtesy Fashion Museum, Bath and North East Somerset Council.)

TEN INTERNATIONAL MUSEUMS WORTH A VISIT

The Victoria and Albert Museum Cromwell Road, London, UK
Fashion Museum Bennett Street, Bath, UK
The Metropolitan Museum of Art 1000 Fifth Avenue (at 82nd Street), New York, USA
Smithsonian Cooper-Hewitt, National Design Museum East 91st Street at Fifth Avenue, New York, USA
Musée du Louvre Louvre, Paris, France
The Musée de la Mode et du Textile Rue de Rivoli, Paris, France
ModeMuseum Provincie Antwerpen (MoMu) Nationalestraat, Antwerp, Belgium
La Triennale di Milano Viale Alemagna, Milan, Italy
Galleria del Costume, Palazzo Pitti, Florence, Italy
The Kyoto Costume Institute (KCI) Shichi-jo Goshonouchi Minamimachi, Kyoto, Japan

Although most museums display a costume court or a dedicated gallery of historic fashion, it is increasingly popular for major designer retrospectives to celebrate the 'art' of fashion within museums; the Giorgio Armani (b.1934) retrospective at the Royal Academy in London (2003) and Yohji Yamamoto's installation at the Victoria and Albert Museum (2011) attracted wide audiences. Alexander McQueen's *Savage Beauty* at New York's Metropolitan Museum of Art in 2011 is the eighth most visited exhibition in the Museum's history (over 660,000 visitors), putting the designer in the same category as previous exhibitions including the treasures of Tutankhamun (1978) and the *Mona Lisa* (1963).

<u>Opposite</u>
To commemorate the Alexander McQueen *Savage Beauty* exhibition at the Metropolitan Museum of Art (2011), renowned New York high-fashion retailer, Bergdorf Goodman, dedicated all of their Fifth Avenue windows to a display of McQueen archival pieces. (Photography courtesy of Maureen Guido.)

<u>Right</u>
Impact: Fifty Years of the CFDA, was on view at The Museum at the Fashion Institute of Technology (MFIT) for over three months in 2012. It showcased 100 garments and accessories designed by the Council of Fashion Designers of America's most impactful designers of the last 50 years. (Photography courtesy MFIT.)

Without doubt, the natural and man-made environments of today are an invaluable resource for researching and developing a designer's critical awareness and should be exploited to the full whenever possible. Historically, the natural world has been an obvious inspiration to artists and designers. From Paleolithic cave painting to the land art of Andy Goldsworthy (b.1956), nature's assets have been utilized for both their decorative value and physical form. They have been a constant muse to generate new and interesting ideas in art and design. Today's engineers and product designers are now applying biomimicry to learn directly from nature in order to make designs more efficient, elegant and sustainable.

'Fashion is not something that exists in dresses only. Fashion is in the sky, in the street, fashion has to do with ideas, the way we live, what is happening.'

Coco Chanel

In addition to the values of shape and structure, one the most informative uses of nature for any fashion designer is its exceptional colour spectrum and textural patterning. The ever-changing seasonal colour palette is a perfect source of natural harmony and balance without any resort to theory or charts. Similarly, the bloom and decay within nature can be the stimulus for all manner of textile structures and fabric embellishments. Alexander McQueen said 'I have always loved the mechanics of nature and to a greater or lesser extent my work is always informed by that.'

PANTONE 7424 C

PANTONE 8021 C

PANTONE 485 C

PANTONE 144 C

PANTONE 7516 C

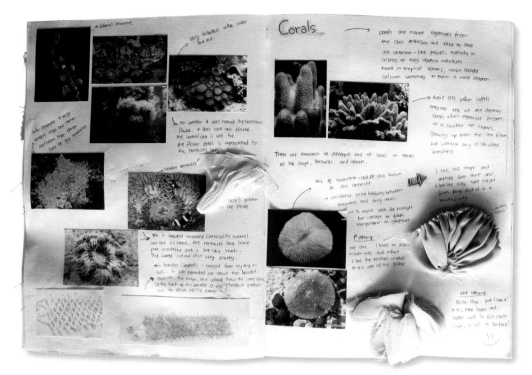

Above
Florentsya (2010)
Cataloguing the natural world in your sketchbook can provide infinite reference material for future design development.

Right
Elvan Otgen (2010)

Opposite
Williamsburg, Brooklyn
The natural environment is a continuous source for inspiring a balanced colour palette.
(Photography © Geoffry Gertz.)

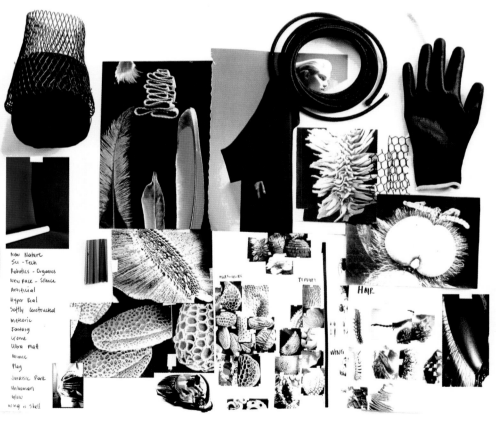

The man-made environment is not unlike the world of fashion itself: it has similarly altered over time and can be easily categorized by its mannerisms and styles from certain periods. Fashion and architecture share a useful symbiotic relationship. They both deal with structure and shape and take the human body as their point of reference. Buildings are identified by their purpose in a similar way to how clothes are labeled by their function and use. The silhouette of a building is often seen mirrored in the dress styles of its era. Interestingly enough, both Pierre Balmain (1914–82) and Gianfranco Ferré (1944–2007) studied architecture. Today's generation of architects have begun to usurp the terminology of the dressmaker (pleating, draping, folding, etc.) while fashion designers are applying the principles of architecture when structuring their garments (Comme des Garçons, Martin Margiela, Hussein Chalayan, and Viktor & Rolf).

The contrasting styles of architecture in urban landscapes are an invaluable source of inspiration and provide cultural clues to a city's heritage and future. The values of silhouette, volume and texture in a building's structure can be easily translated into the language of fashion. The linear streamlined skyscrapers of any modern city skyline, the organic rhythm of Antoni Gaudí's (1852–1926) Barcelona, or the mix of old and new in Beijing provide contrasting approaches in architectural forms that continue to inspire garment design.

Following a visit to New York, Zandra Rhodes' (b.1940) detailed sketchbook drawings of the towering architecture of the city fed directly into her 'Manhattan Collection' that featured the Empire State and Chrysler buildings embroidered in beadwork.

<u>Above</u>
Petronas Twin Towers, Kuala Lumpur, Malaysia
(Photography © Liliana Rodriguez.)
Malaysia's 88-floor skyscrapers, ranked as
the tallest twin buildings in the world, are
typical of the wide variety of dramatic urban
architectural structures that can be easily
mapped onto the construction patterns of
fashion garments.

<u>Below</u>
Casa Milà, Barcelona, Spain
(Photography © Klaus Dolle.)
Antoni Gaudí's undulating stone façade for
Casa Milà ('La Pedrera') is typical of the
distinctive organic architecture that weaves
its way across the city of Barcelona. It
remains a perpetual source of inspiration to
contemporary designers.

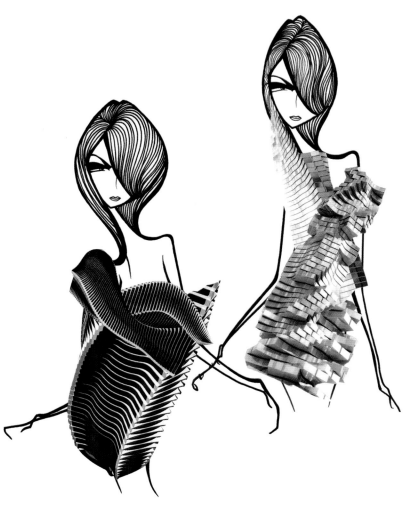

DISTINCTLY DIFFERENT URBAN BUILDINGS
Torre Galatea (Figueres, Spain)
Krzywy Domek (The Crooked House) (Sopot, Poland)
Waldspirale (Forest Spiral) (Darmstadt, Germany)
The Basket Building (Ohio, USA)
Habitat 67 (Montreal, Canada)
Cubic House (Rotterdam, Netherlands)
Dancing Building (Prague, Czech Republic)
Ryugyong Hotel (Pyongyang, North Korea)
Guggenheim Museum (Bilbao, Spain)
Beijing National Stadium (Beijing, China)
Walt Disney Concert Hall (Los Angeles, California, USA)
Atlantis, The Palm Hotel (Dubai, UAE)

TEN UNIQUE WONDERS IN THE NATURAL WORLD
The Great Barrier Reef (Australia)
The Amazon Rainforest (South America)
Yellowstone National Park (Wyoming, Montana, Idaho, USA)
Niagara Falls (Canada/USA border)
Carlsbad Caverns (New Mexico, USA)
The Grand Canyon (Arizona, USA)
Kerepakupai-Meru (Angel Falls) (Venezuela) Venezuela)
The Giant's Causeway (Northern Ireland, UK)
Uluru (Ayers Rock) (Northern Territory, Australia)
Mount Everest and the Himalayas (Nepal/Tibet border, China)

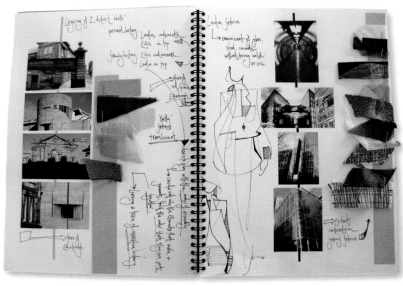

<u>Above</u>
Sandra Azwan (2012)

<u>Below</u>
Louise Bennetts (2012)
The rhythms and patterns of urban architecture,
both ancient and modern, can be easily translated
into garment construction and fabrication ideas.

Secondary sources

Style on the screen: cinema and television

'I saw *Avatar* and, like everyone, found it extraordinary.
And from there I began thinking of nature and ecology, and the Latin
American tropics; and from there it was not very far to Mexico.'

Jean Paul Gaultier

The overlap of fashion with popular mass culture is self-evident. In popular music they even share the same labels (punk, new romantics, grunge, etc.). Cinema and television have had an even more widespread impact upon fashion trends, even outshining those established by the more elite designers of haute couture.

It is a profitable area for the researcher to investigate because of fashion's pronounced integration within the mainstream of mass-media entertainment. Weekly interactions with trendy television shows like *Dynasty*, originally watched during the 1980s through to HBO's *Sex and the City* broadcast from the late 1990s until 2004, projected a total fashion image that was quickly adapted by fashionistas (and designers) around the globe.

Although it is not unknown for fashion designers to cross over and also work in film: Christian Dior for Alfred Hitchcock's (1899–1980) *Stage Fright* (1950); Coco Chanel for Alain Resnais's (b.1922) *Last Year in Marienbad* (1961); Ralph Lauren for *The Great Gatsby* (1974), Giorgio Armani for *American Gigolo* (1980) and *The Untouchables* (1987) and Jean Paul Gaultier for *The Fifth Element* (1997) – cinema prides itself on 'a private' coterie of costume designers that instigate their own fashion styles by dressing movie stars.

The extravagant evening gowns of Adrian (Adolph Greenberg, 1903–59) at MGM in the 1930s and 1940s (also responsible for the red ruby slippers for *The Wizard of Oz*), or the more restrained styles of Edith Head (1897–1981) working over at Paramount and Universal, who was nominated 35 times for Best Costume Design and won eight Academy Awards, are testament to the co-habitation of fashion with film.

Jane Fonda's futuristic *Barbarella* outfits and Gene Roddenberry's (1921–91) *Star Trek* on television made a lasting impact on women's fashions during the 1960s, while in total contrast, Diane Keaton's (b.1946) androgynous tomboy look in *Annie Hall* (1977) styled a look that predominated well into the 1980s. Also in the 1980s, street chic dancewear became the norm due to the popularity of *Fame*, while Tom Cruise (b.1962) and Keanu Reeves (b.1964) made eyewear the key male fashion accessory following *Top Gun* (1986) and *The Matrix* (1999).

Below
Avanti Bidikar (2011)
Mumbai's Hindi-language
Bollywood offers a never-ending
source of colour and invention
for fashion direction.

Fay Millard (2012)
Wizard of Oz
Hollywood is responsible for
providing some of popular culture's
key icons of the 20th century.

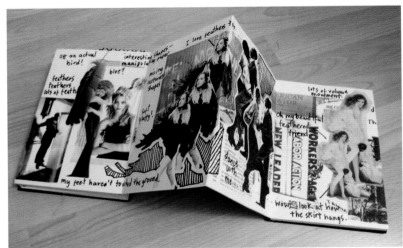

Classic movie idols of the past were the precursors of the celebrity style icons of today and die-hard fans have always attempt to emulate their favourite stars to remain on trend. Veronica Lake's (1922–73) legendary peek-a-boo hairstyle was so universally imitated in the 1940s that she was asked to alter it because it was the cause of accidents in wartime factories. In 1994, an asymmetrically bob-fringed Uma Thurman (b.1970) in Quentin Tarantino's (b.1963) *Pulp Fiction*, assisted in making Chanel's Rouge Noir nail polish a total sell-out for 12 months following the film's release. Sales of women's trousers quadrupled after Katharine Hepburn (1907–2003) famously wore them in *Bringing up Baby* (1938), and in the mid-1950s, white T-shirt sales increased dramatically as a result of James Dean's wardrobe in *Rebel Without a Cause* (1955). James Cameron's (b.1954) *Avatar* not only impacted on Jean Paul Gaultier's Spring 2010 collection but also influenced *Vogue* in a ten-page fashion spread in March 2010. And in 2009 the fashion/film continuum came full circle with Gucci's one-time creative director Tom Ford (b.1961) turning rookie film director with his first movie, *A Single Man*.

Above
Kayleigh Macbeth (2008)
Classic movie icons from celluloid's glamorous past are easy prey for re-invention by contemporary designers.

Opposite
Hannah Dowds (2011)
Film directors such as Alfred Hitchcock, John Ford (1894-1973), Tim Burton (b.1958) and Baz Luhrmann (b.1962) are instantly recognizable by their own metaphoric visual style.

TEN MOVIE FASHION ICONS
Holly Golighty (Audrey Hepburn) in *Breakfast at Tiffany's* (1961)
Bonnie Parker (Faye Dunaway, b.1941) in *Bonnie and Clyde* (1967)
Jennifer Cavalleri (Ali MacGraw, b.1939) in *Love Story* (1970)
Jay Gatsby (Robert Redford, b.1936) in *The Great Gatsby* (1974)
Annie Hall (Diane Keaton) in *Annie Hall* (1977)
Tony Manero (John Travolta, b.1954) in *Saturday Night Fever* (1977)
Julian Kay (Richard Gere, b.1949) in *American Gigolo* (1980)
Karen Blixen (Meryl Streep) in *Out of Africa* (1985)
Susan (Madonna, b.1958) in *Desperately Seeking Susan* (1985)
Carrie Bradshaw (Sarah Jessica Parker, b.1965) in *Sex and the City* (2008)

On the shelf: libraries, books and journals

'Books are a hard-bound drug with no danger of an overdose.
I am the happy victim of books.'

Karl Lagerfeld

There is an old saying that proclaims 'knowledge is free at the library – just bring your own container'. In the age of the World Wide Web, it is too easy for the contemporary designer to dismiss the library as being either outmoded or antiquated.

Today's libraries are undergoing considerable change and the traditional role they once played is developing to keep apace with technology and people's needs and expectations. Historically they were provided to support research, not only as a repository for their vast quantities of books and journals, but also to offer a quiet space in which researchers could work. Almost every town still retains a local public library but it is the larger cities that have established reference libraries that are more beneficial to a designer.

All colleges and universities will have their own dedicated libraries in support of the different programmes that they offer. Art schools that provide a fashion course will usually have a wide variety of archival reference material for access by its current undergraduates: books, periodicals, catalogues, designer files and DVD and digital resources.

Away from academia, specialist archives are often housed within larger public-library and museum complexes, such as the fashion archive of the Victoria and Albert Museum in London, now housed at Blythe House, which includes drawings and fashion plates from the House of Worth dating back to 1889, and The Fashion Group International's immense provision at New York's Public Library, which has fashion-trend reports dating back to 1931.

The older the library, the more likely it is to have those sought after, long out of print books, still available on its shelves. The Lipperheide Kostümbibliothek in Berlin dates back to 1899 and remains one of the oldest fashion-library archives in the world, with over 38,000 books on fashion and clothing and approximately 70,000 fashion images. The largest fashion library in the UK is housed within the London College of Fashion and boasts 57,000 books and over 400 periodicals.

It is the annals of vintage fashion journals that are the strongest magnets for today's researchers into fashion's history. These often-fragile magazine archives are incalculable stores of reference. *Vogue* and *Harper's Bazaar* were the .com windows of their day, cataloging and profiling the newest designers and the latest fashion trends. The chronological photographing and marketing of fashion is vital reference and it remains individually captured and documented for all future researchers.

Although digitization has made the fragile archives even more widely available (every issue of *Vogue* since 1892 is now accessible via subscription to WGSN (Worth Global Style Network), there remains something special about turning the pages of a real magazine in a library's special collection that a computer monitor cannot replicate.

Left
Natalie Johnson (2011)
The tactile quality of
books can also be an
inspiration for a designer
from the unique leather
binding and tooling found
on vintage books to their
regimented arrangement
and organization on
bookcases and shelves.

TEN FASHION LIBRARIES AROUND THE WORLD

Gladys Marcus Library Fashion Institute of Technology (FIT) West 27th Street, New York, USA
London College of Fashion 100 Curtain Road, London, UK
Von-Parish Kostümbibliothek Munich City Museum Sankt-Jakobs-Platz 1, Munich, Germany
June F. Mohler Fashion Library Rockwell Hall, Kent State University, Ohio, USA
Lipperheide Kostümbibliothek Art Library, National Museums of Berlin, Matthäikirchplatz, Berlin, Germany
Adam and Sophie Gimbel Design Library Sheila Johnson Design Centre, 2W 13th St.#2,New York, USA
ModeMuseum Provincie Antwerpen (MoMu) Nationalestraat, Antwerp, Belgium
The Irene Lewisohn Costume Reference Library The Metropolitan Museum of Art 1000 Fifth Avenue (at 82nd Street), New York, USA
Centro di Documentazione Matteo Lanzoni Polimoda International Institute of Fashion Design & Marketing Villa Favard, Via Curtatone, 1, Florence, Italy
FIDM/Fashion Institute of Design & Merchandising South Grand Avenue, Los Angeles, California, USA

'Fashion is too often backwards looking. Look at the current trend for 1920s clothes – what does that have to say about how we live now? Designers should be thinking about shoes you can slip off easily as you walk through x-ray machines at airports. Design should shape the future of our lives.'

Karim Rashid (b.1960)

Left
Charlotte Vieilledent (2011)
A typical forecaster's pin board identifying current trends and styles.

Opposite
Sreejith Sreekumar (2009)
It is vital that forecastesr think globally when gathering in information to feed into their predictions.

KOREA

Substrate

Bright Accents

It is imperative that a fashion designer is not only conversant with historical and current design styles but is also aware of future trends. Predictions about the next season's colour palette or silhouette are obviously crucial but they need to be seen as part of a global transition. The political climate, social trends and progressive technologies all have an impact upon peoples' attitudes and lifestyles, which in turn have a bearing on the clothes they will buy and wear in the future. Tuning into this information frequency is not a full-time activity for the fashion designer, but since fashion has always set its sights towards the future there is an understandable knock-on effect to which contemporary fashion designers need to be receptive.

Bespoke fashion forecasting agencies are the industry source of reference for fashion's future trends. They rely upon a sixth sense to generate accurate, up-to-the-minute intelligence of the latest directional trend forecasts months in advance of the season, with analysis and predictions on color, fabrics, print, embellishments, graphics, shapes, silhouettes and detailing.

Nearly all agencies employ global-trend scouts who seek out the most progressive developments emerging onto the fashion scene. They will cover seasonal trend predictions, street-fashion trends, retail analysis and trade-show reports, backed up with runway photographs and catwalk-trend reports. Using this direct approach they are able to confirm the word out on the street that helps their subscribers to stay ahead of future competition.

The world leaders in online trend analysis are www.wgsn.com, www.stylesight.com and www.trendstop.com. However, the type of detailed information that these companies provide remains too expensive for most researchers.

A more cost-effective way for the resourceful fashion researcher is via the network of specialist magazines that attempt to cover the same ground. Publications such as *Collezioni*, *WeAr*, *Close-Up Runway*, *Trendsetter*, *Fashion Box* and *Viewpoint* are widely available and equally function as monitors of trends. Key distributors of magazine trend information are the mode ... information group that advertise themselves as 'the professionals' first choice'. Since its foundation in 1957, it has become the main specialist supplier of printed material for all types of trend information.

One of the most renowned modern-day fashion soothsayers is Dutch trend forecaster Lidewij (Li) Edelkoort (b.1950). During the 1980s, as well as devising innovative trend forums at the bi-annual *Première Vision* in Paris, she also set up the dynamic network forecasting group, Trend Union. She currently heads up an international think-tank offering made-to-measure services for the fashion industry. and was Identified in 2003 by *TIME* magazine as one of the world's 25 most influential people in fashion. her company Edelkoort Editions produces its own range of visionary trend publications including, *View on Colour*, *Interior View* and *Bloom* which she describes as 'horti-cultural' because it charts the changing trends in flowers and the way that designers use those images.

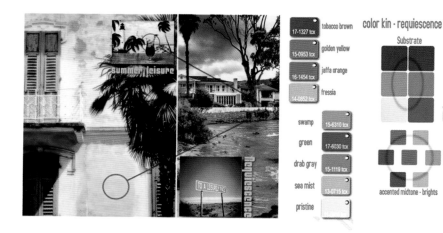

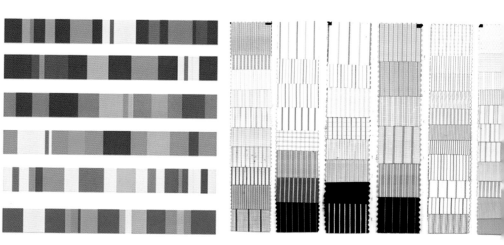

Rachel Lamb (2009)
All forecasters
regard nature as
an unending source
of seasonal colour-
palette inspiration.

Hedera	PANTONE 4625C
Inula	PANTONE 465C
Ajuga	PANTONE 583C
Reseda	PANTONE 222C
Malva	PANTONE 1565C
Crambe	PANTONE 7404C
Senecio	PANTONE 703C
	PANTONE 731C

TEN GLOBAL TREND FORECASTING WEBSITES
EDITD http://editd.com
The Future Laboratory http://thefuturelaboratory.com
The Doneger Group www.doneger.com
Groupe Carlin International www.carlin-international.com
Kjaer Global www.kjaer-global.com
Lidewij Edelkoort www.edelkoort.com
Peclers Paris www.peclersparis.com
Promostyl www.promostyl.com
Trendzine www.fashioninformation.com
WGSN www.wgsn.com

Riffing the fashion information highway: the www and blogosphere

'I can't bear all that over-preciousness of things.
The more things that go out on YouTube live, the better for me.'

Giles Deacon (b.1969)

The easiest (some might argue, the laziest) place to start any research is via the Internet. In less than a generation the networked world has opened up the researching prospects for the designer. Fifty years ago communication was limited to landlines, now without leaving your computer chair, the whole world is accessible from your fingertips. Academics continue to argue the pros and cons of researching via the Internet, but most designers agree that the Internet is preferable because it is convenient, organized and fully accessible.

The Internet has the potential to widen a fashion designer's research capabilities on a specific subject by supplying a more in-depth look at the subject than a current book or journal might provide. Using its many search engines, designers today can easily conduct their investigations at a more accelerated pace. This instant access to information, 24 hours a day, means they can now move more quickly and complete projects faster, compared to hunting down rare books, requesting vintage magazines in a library, or seeking archived items in a museum.

Contemporary fashion attracts an understandably high visibility everywhere online. The firstVIEW website alone currently boasts a fashion database of over four million catwalk-show photographs and videos. While the continued rise of social media sites, like Twitter and Facebook, has meant that images from the latest catwalk shows can now be seen anywhere in the world just minutes after a show finishes – every spectator has turned into a reporter.

Today's fashion bloggers have increasingly become recognized as the frontline of fashion news and worldwide trends. Keen-eyed fashionistas can even outstrip the magazine editors to a fashion headline as they shamelessly share their personal comments and opinions on blogs and forums. By watching these shows, without even needing to be physically present, contemporary bloggers are becoming fashion journalists for the digital age.

Hedi Slimane (b.1968), the creative director for Yves Saint Laurent said, 'The fashion Internet community is like a global digital agora tweeting passions and opinions. Anyone knows better, and each one is a self-made critic.'

A major player among the plethora of available fashion websites is www.SHOWstudio.com. Founded by fashion photographer, Nick Knight (b.1958), it has always championed using digital media in the promotion of fashion. Its streaming of the Alexander McQueen Spring/Summer 2010 fashion show, 'Plato's Atlantis', live from Paris proved so popular that it caused the stream to crash because of the excessive volume of traffic.

London Fashion Week now operates a full digital schedule offering one-site access to all their live streamed shows while www.catwalklive.tv can provide front-row seats at the latest collections from New York, Paris and Milan each season and even tweets 15 minute alerts prior to the commencement of each show. In February 2010 Burberry fully embraced 21st century technology when it became the first major fashion label to stream a catwalk show live across the world in 3D. They are quickly becoming global leaders in the digital fashion stakes and currently invest over 60 per cent of their annual marketing budget into digital media promotion.

Blogs and social networking communities are increasingly useful resources for the researcher because they are driven by private passions that throw up all manner of fascinating insights about their niche subjects. Although their personal views might be one-sided, the depth of their bottom-up shared knowledge can be advantageously exploited. The conveniently hyperlinked presentation and archives of earlier postings can often save a researcher a lot of virtual legwork by suggesting sources and possibilities that might otherwise be overlooked. Undoubtedly, the blogosphere has become an indispensible addition to any fashion researcher's toolkit.

TEN NATIONAL FASHION ORGANIZATION WEBSITES

British Fashion Council - www.britishfashioncouncil.co.uk

Council of Fashion Designers of America - http://cfda.com

Dutch Fashion Foundation - www.dutchfashionfoundation.com

Fashion Design Council of India - www.fdci.org

Fédération Française de la Couture du Prêt-à-Porter desCouturiers and Créateurs de Mode - www.modeaparis.com

Hellenic Fashion Designers Association - http://hfda.gr

Hong Kong Fashion Designers Association - http://www.hkfda.org

Internet Centre for Canadian Fashion & Design - www.ntgi.net/ICCF&D/

Japan Fashion Association - www.japanfashion.or.jp

Nordic Fashion Association - www.nordicfashionassociation.com

TEN STREET FASHION BLOGS BY LOCATION

Barcelona - http:www.lelook.eu

Berlin - http://stilinberlin.blogspot.com

Helsinki - http://www.hel-looks.com

London - http://facehunter.blogspot.co.uk

Milan - http://alltheprettybirds.blogspot.co.uk

Moscow - http://www.slickwalk.com

New York - http://thesartorialist.com

Paris - http://www.garancedore.fr

Sydney - http://www.xssatstreetfashion.com

Tokyo - http://www.style-arena.jp

TEN INTERNATIONAL FASHION INFORMATION WEBSITES

www.catwalklive.tv

www.fashion.net

www.fashionoffice.org

www.firstview.com

www.hintmag.com

www.infomat.com

www.manchic.com

www.SHOWstudio.com.

www.style.com

vintagefashionguild.org

TEN FASHION SOCIAL NETWORKS

www.avenue7com

www.chictopia.com

www.fashionising.com

www.fashionmash.nl

www.onsugar.com

www.polyvore.com

http://styledon.com

www.stylehive.com

www.stylemob.com

http://trendmill.com

Sketchbook task

'Family faces are magic mirrors. Looking at people who belong to us, we see the past, present and future.'

Gail Lumet Buckley (b.1937)

Style roots: discover your own fashion past

Investigating a family's history and creating a family tree has become very popular. Television programmes delve into the ancestry of celebrities, magazines share ways to trace a family's lineage, and the Internet is littered with all manner of freely accessible genealogical records from birth and marriage certificates to immigration and census details. Together these can assist any enthusiast on their quest.

As an alternative to the traditional diagrammatic framework, usually expressed as dates with linked family names, here is an engaging task to build up your own visual alternative, with a specific focus on how your personal fashion sense has been influenced by that of your own family and friends. Every family has albums or shoeboxes with archived photographs ranging from formal family gatherings, like weddings, through to relaxed holiday snaps. They not only preserve memories of those family members but also capture the historical context of the events by showing changing styles of dress across successive generations. Even the type of camera used and the photographs produced represent a barometer of the prevailing style of the time, from the 'staged' conformity of yesteryear framed for posterity, to the immediacy of the contemporary camera-phone picture posted on Facebook.

1. Locate as many photographs showing your family as possible. At first it is best not to discriminate too much. You will doubtless find lots of recent examples but try to seek out earlier photographs by going as far back as your grandparents at least. By keeping to your own family you should be able to trace how they are dated and sequenced. Arrange your photographs in chronological order and prepare a selection that has personal meaning and interesting style characteristics. Make duplicates of your selection to protect the originals.

2. Now think of a creative way to gather together and display your photographs as a record of your own fashion style roots. Don't go for the obvious – be inventive. You might reduce or enlarge their physical size, cut into them, or paint or decorate the subject to highlight specific areas. Whatever you do, you should always aim to retain the genealogical value of the originals when establishing your revamped family tree.

3. Make sure you represent all your activity within your sketchbook by showing your progression as well as the final display.

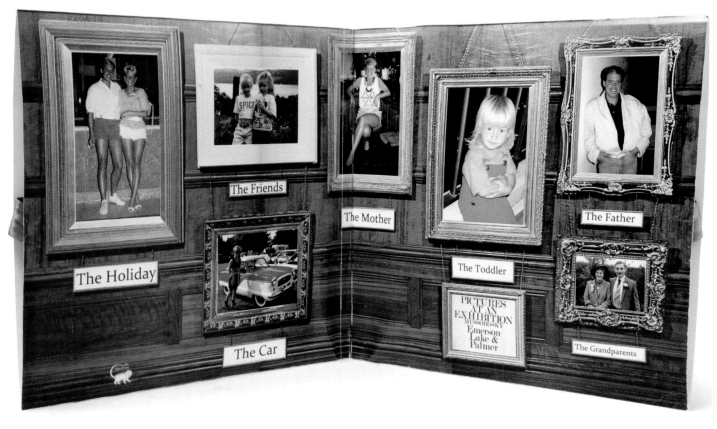

Right and opposite
Jade Barrett (2012)
'I adapted the cover of an
old vinyl LP as my final
display board. I chose to
include the older photos of
my nan and grandad because
this represented the 1950s
era and I have always liked
the fashion during that
decade. The majority of the
photos are of my mum and dad
since they inevitably became
the main influence on my own
fashion style when I was
growing up.'
(Photography © Dave
Schofield.)

Sketchbook task

'Picture postcards really excite me.'

Henry Miller (1891–1980)

'Wsh u wr hr!': prescriptive stitch

In an age of instant email, texting, Skype and social networking, the concept of writing and sending a postcard from a holiday destination is an endangered pastime. However, postcards were once the most popular means of sending home a snapshot keepsake of one's travels. Today, the hassle of purchasing a local stamp and tracking down a postbox is out of kilter with current demands for instant and convenient digital communication.

Postcards were first issued in the UK around 1870 as plain cards both front and back, and were purchased pre-stamped. These were followed in 1894 by one-sided picture postcards that sparked their golden age between 1902 and the First World War in 1914, when it became a national craze, with millions of picture postcards being sent. The embroidered postcards that emerged during the First World War are often known as 'WW1 Silks' because they were hand-embroidered by female French and Belgium refugees onto strips of mesh prior to mounting onto the postcard.

Previously it had also been popular to overstitch existing photographs with decorative embroidery; European national costume was a popular choice and Spanish flamenco dancers and toreadors were obvious choices for embellishment. This quaint convention can make an amusing task that will bring tactile decoration into your fashion sketchbook.

Left
Vintage Spanish postcards decorated with embroidery stitches.

Opposite
GLTZ/ Embroidery (2010)
Contemporary application of embroidery in fashion photography.
Aušra Osipavičiūtė (photography)
Milda Čergelytė (fashion)
Gintarė Pašakarnytė (embroidery)
Greta Babarskaitė (make-up)
Greta and Vaclovas (models)

1. Locate a striking figurative photograph from a magazine. Size will also be an important consideration. A normal rectangular postcard is between 9 x 13cm (3½ x 5in) and 15 x 30cm (6 x 11½in). Glue your image to an existing postcard, or lightweight card, to give the image sufficient body to withstand your embroidery. Remember that you will be making rows of holes in the image and it may easily perforate if it is not stable enough.

2. Decide which areas of the figure you are going to embellish with stitch. You might want to test out some stitches before working directly onto your postcard. Don't overwork the image – there should be enough of the original to maintain the original mood. You can work either by hand or at a sewing machine, depending on the quality you require. Always allow your personality to influence your decoration, thread, yarn or stitch choices. As you will be fixing the final postcards into your sketchbook there is no need to clean up the reverse of the postcard. Attaching fabric or decorating with sequins is another option.

3. Attach the finished postcards into your sketchbook.

Showcase 2

Name:
Studio Codex (by Mendie Karagantcheff)
Nationality:
Dutch
Graduate:
Royal Academy of Arts,
The Hague,
The Netherlands
Collection 2012-13:
'Generation Overload'

'My sketchbooks are worth a million bucks to me. For each collection they are like a personal bible – a sacred writing – also known as 'codex'. Sketching allows me to create an ambiance and experience for the collection that can be seen as the core of my work. That is also why I work by the name of Studio Codex.

I prefer working in a sketchbook with a ring binder. That way it allows the book to grow with the addition of lots of material. Following a period of complete creative chaos the book almost bursts and weighs about three times as much as it did when it was empty.

My ideas always develop while working in my sketchbook. I use techniques such as collage, drawing, mind mapping and collecting interesting literature and fabric/material samples. Music is also a huge part of the process; it really get's me into the necessary state of mind. The experience helps to visually shape the ideas inside my head; once 'in the flow', it's unstoppable.

Without this visual foundation I'm unable to design. You could say that the clothing is subordinate to the sketching – that's the most important thing.

I often work from archetypal aspects. The departure point for my 'Generation Overload' collection was Carl Jung's 'persona'. My interest lies in the way that we communicate today – usually online. Everything is great, fun, bigger, better, even fantastic, and everybody 'likes' it. It is fascinating how we project ourselves to the world and how we continue our 'online façade' in our offline lives. We are literally living in our own app-culture. Using my sketchbook I started to visualize and associate all the different aspects that have created the current (online) youth culture. It's not just about calling someone on your iPhone, it's about filming, uploading pictures, listening to music, texting, tweet-ing, like-ing, ping-ing, swipe-ing and using all sorts of apps to comfort our daily life. This aspect will also continue through into the collection. It's not just about clothing, it's about the whole experience. The clothing will be subordinate to the interactive (such as apps, films, music) and graffiti (such as prints, animation) elements of this collection, and hopefully everyone will be wanting to join the club: the Codex Club.'

I always take my inspiration from my personal surroundings. There is a strong environmental focus within my designs that people should be able to relate and identify with.'

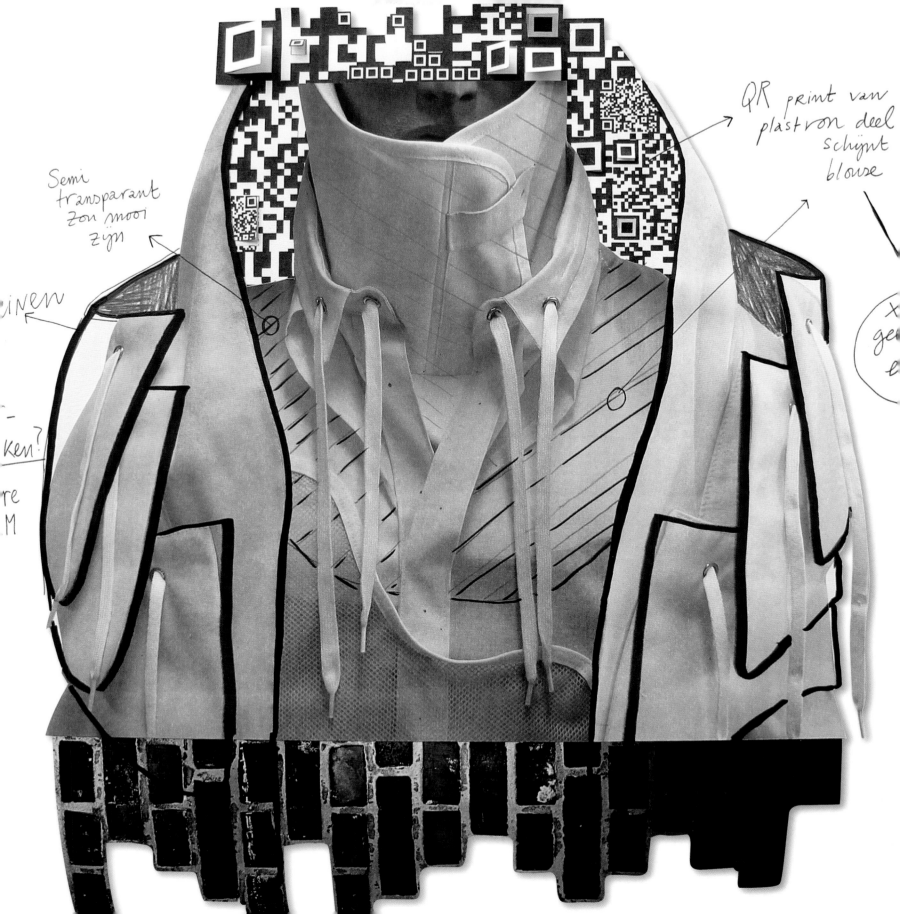

Semi
transparant
zou mooi
zijn

...inen

...ken?

...re
M

QR print van
plastron deel
schijnt
blouse

Keuzevrijheid is geen beperking
maar een mogelijkheid tot

opeenstapeling
opeenstapeling
opeenstapeling
opeenstapeling
opeenstapeling

en sculpturale
silhouetten
en vormen.

OPEENSTAPELING
LEIDT TOT
NIEUWE
VORMEN

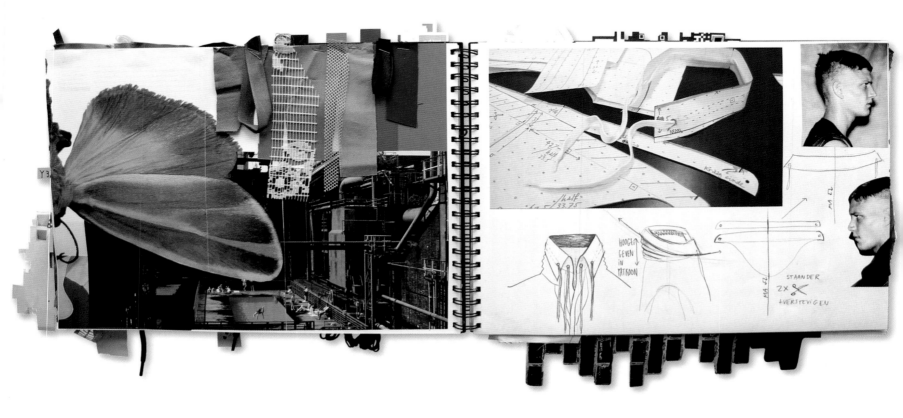

HOOGTE
GEVEN
IN
PATROON

STAANDER
2X
+VERSTEVIGEN

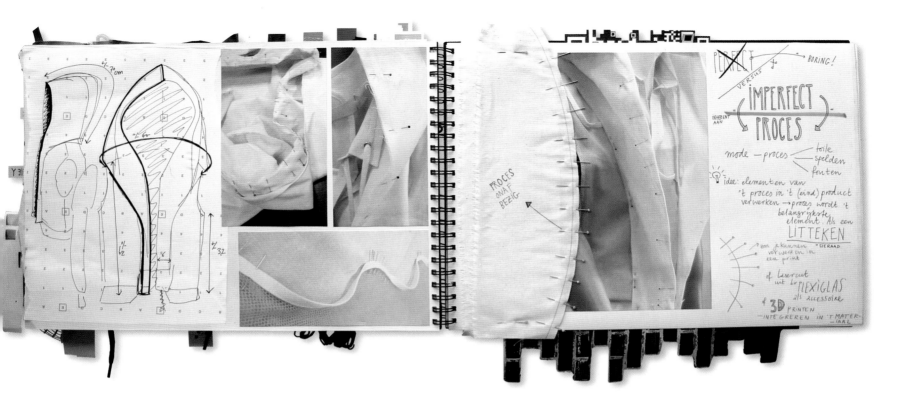

PERFECT ↗ BORING!
versus
IMPERFECT
inherent aan → PROCES ←

mode — proces ⟨ toile
                   spelden
                   fouten

💡 idee: elementen van
't proces in 't (eind) product
verwerken → proces wordt 't
belangrijkste element. Als een
LITTEKEN

• zou je kunnen •SIERAAD
verwerken in
een print

of laseruut uit bv PLEXIGLAS
als accessoire

• 3D PRINTEN
- INTEGREREN IN 'T MATER-
                        -IAAL

PROCES
ONAF
BEZIG →

"EEN DAG NIETS GEPOST
IS EEN DAG NIET GELEEFD"
+1 Add as Friend

TOM 22
1990
👍 14

→ dit is een vlinder!

CHAPTER 3

Visual thinking: evaluation and appraisal

'Design is thinking made visual.'

Saul Bass (1920–96)

Chapter 1 introduced you to the main ingredients of the research necessary for inclusion in your fashion sketchbook. Chapter 2 pointed you towards various primary and secondary resources that can help you to find reference material. In this chapter you will now begin to evaluate your findings as possible springboards towards eventual designs. A fashion sketchbook must never be allowed to remain as a scrapbook: it is a personal store cupboard full of indispensable information that will need to be expanded in order for it to ignite new design ideas and concepts.

It is now time to survey your visual cache to see where it can lead you. A fashion sketchbook is like an explorer's map, with an 'X' marking the spot where the treasure is waiting to be uncovered.

By directing your personal visual enquiries towards your assembled research you will be able to steer it away from the known towards the new and inventive. It is about opening your mind and thinking differently. Don't fall into the trap of accepting everything at face value – you need to apply some lateral thinking as well.

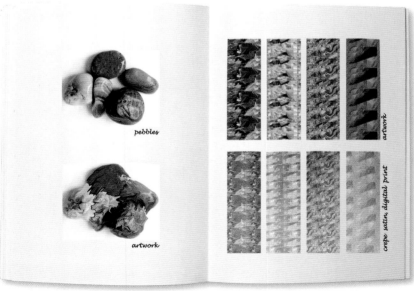

Unlike a mathematician or scientist who would accept the idea that 1+1=2, for a designer that result would be too obvious; it lacks the missing values of imagination and creativity that should have resulted in 1+1=3. This magical outcome cannot be explained mathematically, but designers set their sights on it because in the end it is the correct answer. It is a personal and intuitive process that is completely different with each designer. Everyone can recognize it when they see it but it is very difficult to formalize into a set of rules or instructions.

In the previous chapter you saw how it is just as important to look away from fashion in order to bring something new to the table. Sometimes it is difficult to view your research with fresh eyes. In gathering the information together you can become too easily attached to its origins and beginnings. Obviously you do not want to discard the primary value of your research – that is why you chose it in the first place – but to use it too literally will only limit its future appeal. A seam for seam copy of a garment can appear corny and come across more like a painstaking task of homage rather than a tribute to the original's merit as inspiration. In the design world of today, where inevitably nothing is new any more, designers are under persistent pressure to reinvent the known and juxtapose their findings to generate new possibilities.

The first skill of any fashion designer is not in their dexterity with scissors and pins (that comes later) but in their ability to analyze initial design research in order to challenge convention and create something new. The originality of the idea is always in the interpretation of the initial research: putting unexpected colours together; straightening curves into diagonals; inflating or shrinking shapes; turning things upside down – these are all tried and tested methods of drawing attention to a new design. You will need to learn to chart your own distinct course through your assembled research in order to achieve your personal aspirations.

This chapter will introduce some basic methods of surveying and expanding your thinking and research by mind mapping, collage, juxtaposition, deconstruction, contextualization and establishing a concept.

Connecting the unconnected: mind mapping

Because of the distinctive nature of their specialism, designers can all too easily get stuck within certain thinking patterns. It is sometimes difficult to step away and look afresh at your subject because as a designer you are typically living, eating and drinking it 24/7. An effective method of breaking through these thought patterns and unscrambling them in order to generate new ideas is via the brainstorming process of mind mapping or idea mapping. It helps to work off the cuff and become totally spontaneous in your mind mapping. Connections don't need to be too obvious – often the more quirky the association, the better the idea prompt. It is a powerful tool to free up the mind and to track your ideas.

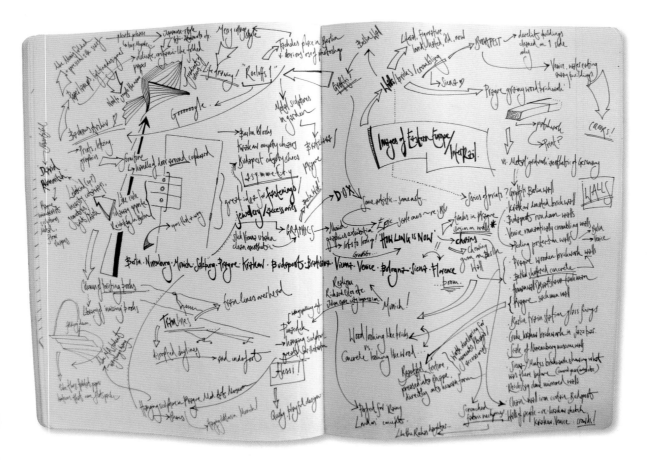

'When I want to do something analytical, I make a list. When I'm trying to come up with ideas or strategize, I make a mind map. Mind maps are organic and allow me to free associate. They are great for asking questions and revealing connections between seemingly unrelated ideas. I start in the center with the issue or problem I am working on and then as I move farther away I get better and better ideas as I force myself to follow the branches on the map and in my mind. The cool thing is that you allow yourself to follow your inner thoughts, which is different than making a list where you are trying to be complete and deal with data.'

David M. Kelley (b.1951)

Your research will already have resulted in numerous images that will benefit from this type of focused exercise. Mind mapping is like an intricate web of thoughts that will trigger your imagination to take an idea, thought or even a single word or image and by association start to connect the unconnected.

Visually it can often resemble a family-tree chart with swelling branches of progeny. However, you don't need to worry too much about its overall diagrammatic structure – it will evolve in its own way depending upon how the mind map grows. Designers predictably find it a liberating experience because it can free up their creativity and generate new areas for consideration that are not always apparent at first glance.

Many designers centre a word or image on the page, but this is not necessary just as long as there is room to add more links as your creative juices start to flow. It is usually restricted to one side of a piece of paper or open sketchbook, used in landscape orientation, to make the associations easier to follow as a holistic exercise. Usually better and better ideas suggest themselves the further away you go from the original starting point.

Opposite
Louise Bennetts (2011)

Right
Studio Codex (by Mendie Karagantcheff) (2012)
Designers usually develop their own personal style of mind mapping. Images are also useful ingredients within the radiating web of information. Because designers use visuals to prompt their ideas, mind mapping transcends being merely a word-association game. You can even carry out multiple mind maps that will bounce off each other. Don't be afraid to use different fonts and colours to add weight and show associations within your train of thoughts.

The shape of change: collage

Designers often use the phrase 'happy accident' when they are generating new ideas. Some of their best thoughts often occur by chance; when a series of unrelated elements inadvertently come together to generate something completely new and unexpected. Designers must allow for the unexpected within their output and serendipity plays a key part in the creative process of designing. Because of fashion's compulsion every six months to throw out the old and welcome in the new, such unplanned events work directly in a fashion designer's favour.

> 'Collage is the twentieth century's greatest innovation.'
>
> Robert Motherwell

A tried-and-tested way to trigger this inspirational state of affairs in fashion design is to use the technique of hand collage. Whether it is by luck or the creative mind searching for new possibilities, collage is a great way to 'play' with your visual research and to test out what might result without ever devaluing any of its potential. By adopting a simple process of pasting various structures together you will effectively be shedding new light upon the possible future direction of your research in terms of silhouette, texture and colour. Collage is a quick and easy shortcut to expanding your reference with almost immediate results. It will help you to explore new ideas, encourage original objectives and develop interesting concepts for your research. However, the purpose of collage in the fashion sketchbook is not simply to decorate the original source; with practice you will be able to use collage to build up your own personal language and acquire a special visual vocabulary through which to articulate your own ideas and concepts.

However rudimentary it might have first appeared, collage has had a significant and important lineage within the story of modern art and design.

It might not have always been recognized by its current idiom but as a technique collage has been around for a very long time. Early cavemen may have been the first exponents by adding seeds, shells and feathers onto their cave paintings, but by the 12th century Japanese calligraphers were fastidiously gluing paper and fabric together to create a decorative background for their poems.

The word originates from the French verb *coller* meaning 'to glue'. In the 18th century, lace valentine greetings and butterfly-wing collages began to appear, and throughout the 19th century all manner of printed scraps, photographs and mementos were being pasted on to a multitude of available surfaces. As well as being trapped within keepsake books, hand collage also flourished on screens, lampshades and household furnishings. In a more ordered way, the art of patchwork is akin to collage where stitch replaces glue.

In its contemporary form, collage developed during the early part of the 20th century as a technique used by Cubist painters Georges Braque (1882–1963), Pablo Picasso and Juan Gris (1887–1927), as a way of explaining their early artistic experiments. They started attaching foreign materials such as cloth, labels, postage stamps, sheet music and wallpaper onto their existing paintings much to the displeasure of the art critics who viewed it as a form of cheating.

Collage also emerged as an important component with key painters and designers working during the later Futurist, Constructivist, Surrealist and Pop Art movements. Richard Hamilton's (1922–2011) *Just What Is It That Makes Today's Homes So Different, So Appealing?* cut from a vintage American *Ladies' Home Journal* magazine in 1956, was the first collage to really achieve true iconic status. Early posters in theatres and cinemas also used collage techniques to assemble and frame their coming attractions.

Of all the 20th century art movements, it was the reactionary Dadaists who made the fullest use of the potential of collage in their work. For many it became their primary means of artistic expression and a means of subverting the original context of the images. Some Dada artists allowed the random chance of arrangement within their compositions to take place by pasting torn paper as and where it fell on to the page. Kurt Schwitters (1887–1948), who is widely considered to be the father of modern collage, famously recycled the contents of his waste paper basket and used these *objets trouvés* to resurrect the throw-away and worthless and turn it into something new and emotive (Mertz).

He famously extended his recycled picture-making activities by converting his parents' house into a 'Merzbau' by totally re-covering the interior walls and ceilings with 3D constructivist shapes that formed nooks and crannies that he filled with found objects. Schwitters said 'What the material meant before its use in a work of art is of no importance.'

Other artists were forced to employ collage in their work because of personal circumstances. During the First World War, French painter Ferdinand Léger (1881–1955) resorted to using cartridge boxes in his artwork because of the lack of paper on the front lines, and a bedridden Henri Matisse (1869–1954) was forced to abandon his paintbrush during his final years and start drawing with scissors and coloured paper cut-outs instead.

Left
Misha Lucie Hannah Edwards (2012)
Collage can often result in thought-provoking assemblies that challenge perception by distorting the expected in the manner of the classic Surrealist/Dada artists like Giorgio de Chirico (1888-1978) and Max Ernst (1891-1976).

Opposite
Sumbal Tariq (2012)
The simple rearrangement of cut-outs can playfully increase a myriad of unexplored avenues for design development. American author, Donald Barthelme (1931-89) observed that 'The principle of collage is the central principle of all art in the twentieth century'.

Despite hand collage's celebrated artistic heritage, it remains as relevant today as it ever was. The impact of digitization and the ready availability of imagery at image-hosting websites such as Flickr, points towards even more collage-related applications (photomontage and image manipulation) in the future. Physically cutting out imagery and pasting it down manually is being replaced by clicking the cut and paste commands of digital software.

David Hockney's (b.1937) fascination with photography has resulted in him bringing technology and collage closer together in his very large and stimulating 'joiners' that almost resemble Cubist compositions in their structured layering. Collage techniques are also being practiced in contemporary music, poetry and film.

As well as the attraction of the individual image shapes and their content, hand collage in the fashion sketchbook can also bring into play a useful tactile element. The textures of antique paper stock, old photographs, shinny buttons, pressed flowers or delicate lace can all increase the collagist's box of tricks. The layering possibilities also allow you to use transparency effects to further open up creative possibilities.

The range of promising ingredients for a successful collage is never-ending. It is subject only to the limitations imposed on it by the designer's own imagination and visual flare. Vintage art, consumer culture, retro iconography, mixed media and recycled urban imagery are all easy prey for the contemporary collagist. However, just as a traditional painter needs to select judiciously from his colour palette, it is also important to keep an aesthetic eye on the outcomes of your collage making. Happy accidents should be encouraged and will happen quite naturally, but it is equally important not to let the collage degenerate into a meaningless assembly of shapes and textures.

Opposite, left
Faye Millard (2012)

Opposite, centre
Ross Williams (2011)

Opposite, right
Alexander Romaniewicz (2012)

Right
Xiaoping Huang (2012)
Collage has effortlessly migrated from the hand-cut into the virtual and freely embraced the digital medium. Digitization has introduced even more potential for expanding the technique of collage by employing software filters and effects to further alter the arranged imagery.

Disruption to order: juxtaposition

Mental association acts as a prompt to the brain to help us understand or appreciate things by their connections. Throughout our lives we unconsciously make thousands of mental associations and suggestions based upon the experiences we have: it might be hearing a piece of music that suddenly triggers recollections of a different time or place, or meeting up with an old friend that conjures up childhood emotions and memories. In Chapter 1 you learned about how certain colour associations have become so closely combined in our subconscious that it is now almost impossible to detach them: baddies always wear black and red invariably warns of danger.

But what happens when this relationship is challenged and the safety net is removed, causing the known to become the unknown?

'Creativity is that marvelous capacity to grasp mutually distinct realities and draw a spark from their juxtaposition.'

Max Ernst

Opposite
Titarubi (2008)
Surrounding David
An 8.5m (28ft) high fibreglass 'David', ornamented in handmade brocade, is dramatically juxtaposed with the original in Florence.

Left
Electric Skins'
(Night Festival 2008)
Australian group,
The Electric Canvas,
transformed the façade of the National Museum of Singapore into a giant chalk sketch against a night sky blackboard by using a projected overlay.
(Both images courtesy of the National Museum of Singapore.)

Image correlation is a powerful tool of suggestion within any designer's lexicon of creativity. It can augment the synthesis of disassociated components by virtue of the new combinations and placements that are produced. Its impact is based around the enhanced interpretation that this juxtaposition of initially dissimilar things is capable of suggesting in their new arrangement. The result might be beautifully attractive, as in Indonesian artist, Titarubi's brocade-covered re-interpretation of Michelangelo's *David* (see left); but it might also be the cause for distaste and repulsion as in UK art terrorist, Banksy's (b.1974) controversial poster image for his 2009 Summer Exhibition in his home town of Bristol, by the juxtaposition of a dropped ice-cream cone sitting atop a pile of dog mess decorated with sprinkles.

To a designer, this is when 'juxtapose' becomes 'just suppose ...'. By removing the preconceived, a designer makes the viewer reconsider the values of the original in the context of the new. You see it in a fresh light. In an industry like fashion, where the one constant is the human frame, juxtaposition makes the finite infinite.

Unlike Chinese artist Liu Bolin (b.1973), who meticulously camouflages himself into his immediate surroundings using paint, juxtaposing an alternative skin for any fashion designer is the opportunity to re-dress the given figure and present an original statement.

Modern advertising exploits juxtaposition as part of its creative building blocks by conjuring up powerful and original visual metaphors. An all-too familiar example is the recurring juxtaposing of fast cars with jungle cats to suggest that the product possesses comparable qualities of speed, power and endurance.

However, some of the ad campaigns' rhetoric is not always as logical. Combining more off-the-wall or risqué promotional imagery is becoming the industry standard: in 1998, wave crests that morphed into white stallions were used to promote the Irish beer, Guinness; while in 2007 Cadbury's Dairy Milk chocolate was publicized by the drumming antics of a gorilla.

Predictably for fashion, product marketing continues to test the limits on what is acceptable and attractive by those who are seeking to make an impact. Fashion label United Colors of Benetton used their own brand of shock tactics to juxtapose fashion with issues in contemporary society. The innocence of the colourful Italian knitwear label was forever shattered by the hard-hitting social commentary provided by Oliviero Toscani's (b.1942) photography used worldwide in their billboard campaigns. Images of the deathbed of an HIV positive patient in hospital; Pope Benedict XVI kissing Ahmed el-Tayeb, imam of the al-Azhar Mosque in Cairo, Egypt, or a bloodied, newly born baby girl still attached by her umbilical cord, provoked some of the most censured visuals of any advertising campaign.

Unlike collage, a rearrangement by juxtaposition doesn't necessarily rely upon a multiple fragmentation to generate it effect. It can easily be achieved by simply placing different things side-by-side, either for comparison or contrast, to communicate a new understanding. Neither does it involve removing items from their original context and reassembling them to create something physically different in their new arrangement. Juxtaposition is there to provide the initial spark that prompts an alternative reaction caused by the association of previously unrelated things. It directs their new relationship towards creating a fresh viewpoint and stimulus for design.

The incentive for ashion designers in employing juxtapositions within their sketchbooks is the celebration of this visual coalition. They can discover and promote either similarities or differences through a continuous train of thought. By bringing items together in this way, designers are able to expand the potential of their original qualities. Connections that may not have been all that obvious before might result from comparisons in scale, shape, colour, texture or pattern. Wild and excessive mark making can be thrown into a new perspective by being trapped within a controlled and formal structure. Geometric, urban architecture might rub shoulders with organic natural forms or the microscopic can be fascinatingly offset when shown adjacent to gigantic proportions. Tender with tough, wet with dry, hot with cold – the possibilities are endless.

Because they are detached from their original context, juxtapositions can appear at first glance misplaced and puzzling – a disruption to the normal order of things. Designers often apply confusing juxtapositions in their work with the full knowledge that whoever receives the information will have to work out the connection for themselves.

Juxtaposition is also a favourite ploy of the trend forecaster who uses the impact and simplicity of the combination to add new meaning to colour, fabric, shape and detailing predictions. The ability to forecast trends depends on exploring contexts and defining new relationships within each creative field. By juxtaposing simple visual fragments in this way, the forecaster has a clear-cut tool to assist in explaining his or her vision cleanly and swiftly to clients.

Through arranging selected imagery from their investigative research that reiterates a distinctive shape or repeats a particular colouring, forecasters are able to predict the emergence of a trend or direction in an easy to understand language. The information can be directly expressed and be totally explicit in its meaning or alternatively be more subtle and suggestive.

Because it is primarily visual, there are no language barriers to the information. It can be accepted at its face value and then be decoded and used by the industry. Juxtaposition has many applications in the world of fashion. Its primary function is to bring new associations and relationships between existing things. This is vital in fashion design where the same components are endlessly repeated. Juxtaposition in the fashion sketchbook has the ability to instigate examination of the known and to provide a direction for future focus, whether via corresponding harmonies or confrontational clashes, in order to make the ideas less literal and the designs more thought provoking.

Below
Rosa Ng (2011)

Opposite
Eleanor Mountfort
(2009)
It is the alignment
of previously
unrelated items
that makes the act
of juxtaposition
so interesting and
profitable for a
fashion designer. By
shifting the context,
the new association
will inevitably
lead to a different
understanding and
fresh appreciation.

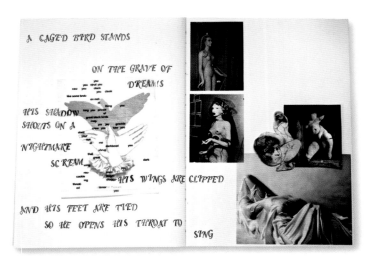

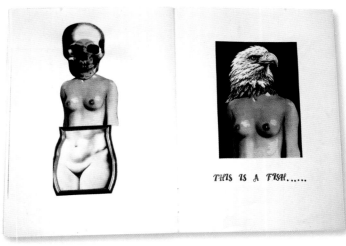

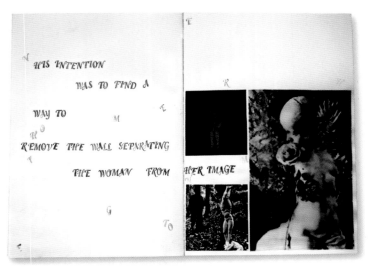

As in Surrealist art, the juxtaposition of ideas contradicts with the familiarity of the real world. The Surrealists' attraction to juxtaposition also exploited scale, placement and emphasis, making the relationships between objects appear unusual and out of the ordinary.

Elsa Schiaparelli (1890–1973) always enjoyed the irrationality and notoriety that juxtaposition could bring to her fashion designs.

For her Autumn/Winter 1937–38 collection she worked alongside another surrealist artist, Salvador Dalí (1904–89), to create a piece of wearable fashion art in the form of her notorious 'Shoe Hat'. Reputedly inspired by a photograph of Dalí wearing one of his wife's slippers perched on top of his head, the upturned high-heel shoe corresponded perfectly with the curvature of the head. They collaborated further on 'The Lobster Dress', which was conspicuously worn by the American socialite, Wallis Simpson (1896–1986), in the series of fashion plates by Cecil Beaton (1904–80). She worked again with Dalí the following season on her 'Tears Dress', as part of her 'Circus' collection that featured *trompe l'oeil* fabric rips printed directly onto the gown. The same collection boasted the famous 'Skeleton Dress' that used raised, padded sections to mimic the wearer's underlying skeletal backbone, ribcage and leg bones.

Over 70 years later, Jean Paul Gaultier produced his own variation with his 'Skeleton Corset', notoriously worn by Dita Von Teese (b.1972) at his Autumn/Winter 2010 fashion show in Paris. During the 1980s Gaultier had already pioneered the use of lingerie as outerwear – a look made famous by Madonna wearing conical bras and ultra-tight girdles over existing clothes during her 'Blond Ambition' tour in the early 1990s.

Schiaparelli went on to work with the French avant-garde artist and film-maker, Jean Cocteau (1889–1963), and reused some of his very individual drawings embroidered onto several of her garments, including the likeness of a woman's cascading golden hair reproduced full length onto the right sleeve of a evening jacket. As executed by the Lesage embroiderers with hindsight it now seems an obvious image placement.

Left
Linzie Reid (2011/12)

Opposite
Alexander Romaniewicz (2012)
The Surrealist Movement's attempts to change our perceptions of the rational and to liberate the imagination are ideal ingredients for translation into contemporary fashion design.

The art of reinvention: deconstruction

'How fashionable to wear clothes that are distressed. The young on the Westside of Los Angeles dress themselves in jeans worn, sanded, and razored to resemble something a six-month castaway might crawl ashore in.'

David Mamet (b.1947)

These days, it is nothing out of the ordinary to see the widespread evidence of garments incorporating raw edges, exposed seams and distressed fabrics out on the fashion high street. Less than a generation ago this would never have been sanctioned as even being on the fashion agenda.

Given that fashion prides itself on its appearance it might at first seem inappropriate that retailers would give hanger space to deconstruction as a selling point. These 'Emperor's New Clothes' tactics seem out of kilter with fashion's traditional heritage of perfection at all costs. By the same token you wouldn't contemplate buying damaged items at an electrical store or car showroom.

The current fascination with all things vintage doesn't allow for damaged goods either. Whether it is 1930s retro furniture or a Cath Kidston (b.1958) rehash of 1950s florals, it is more about the quality of the preservation of the original and certainly not about its decay. So why has deconstruction become a consideration for fashionistas? It's almost as if the routine values of quality and beauty are being turned upside down.

Right
Shabira Dowley (2011)
Deconstruction gives a different aesthetic to garments by suggesting alternative values of beauty beyond the traditional.

Opposite
Jousianne Propp (2011)
Tailoring is a multi-layered technique in garment construction that rewards detailed investigation to expose its hidden structure.

By giving garments an unfinished appearance, today's designers are purposefully drawing attention to the actual craft of their art and the inherent development process of design. Distressed clothing reveals an awareness of their knowledge and understanding. It is each designer's intention to challenge the long-standing perception that garments must be flawlessly finished in order to be admired or even considered beautiful. They are attempting to draw out the hidden meanings behind their clothes by exposing their construction.

Using deconstruction methods within your sketchbook will enable you to stand back from your research and reflect upon its value from a completely different standpoint. The deconstruction of your research will unlock its latent design potential as if you were breaking up a completed jigsaw puzzle. It will allow you to see all the interlocking parts that make up the whole and to evaluate them on their own terms.

The Haynes *Owner's Workshop Manuals* that depict a strip-down/rebuild formula, are typical of the deconstruct/reconstruct approach used by today's fashion designers in order to formulate new designs and ideas. Taking garments back to their roots reveals potential for any future reconstruction of the individual parts.

A person's facial features or idiosyncrasies may not conform to traditional ideals of beauty or standards of good behaviour, but often single them out for special attention. Freckles might be biologically acknowledged as a skin blemish but it doesn't automatically follow that a person with freckles is deemed ugly. Similarly with fashion, a ripped hole or frayed edge in a garment shouldn't therefore be regarded as a sign of unattractiveness. It is the distinctive features of a garment that mark it out as being unique or special. They provide the character of a piece – the device that makes it distinctive and original.

However, cheating with deconstruction should be frowned upon. If a garment has been manufactured to appear weathered and torn then it should not be given the accolade of deconstruction. It has to be truly authentic to impart its essential meaning.

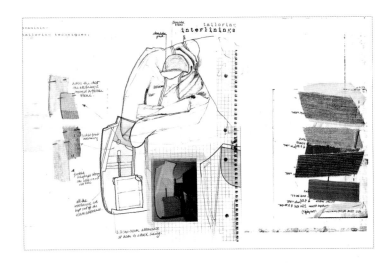

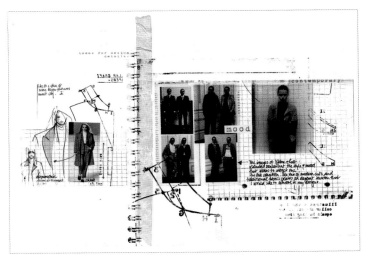

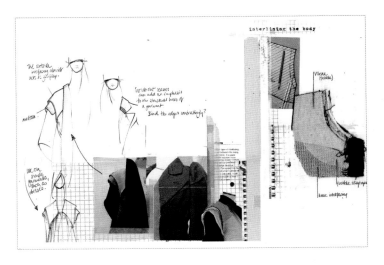

This recent propensity for people to dress in distressed clothes is nothing new. The 'make-do-and-mend' aesthetic of wartime austerity became a feature of the first wave of deconstruction in 20th century fashion – punk. With their emphasis on worn and altered garments, devotees of punk in 1970s' London headed towards a small shop on the fringes of the King's Road in Chelsea called 'SEX'.

The guiding principle for all punks was to break away from what they viewed as an over-marketed and manufactured society. It was their purpose to start a new youth culture as different from the mainstream as they could make it. To achieve this they purposely deviated from what was acceptable in music, hairstyles and clothing. Run by Vivienne Westwood and Malcolm McLaren (1946–2010), the boutique spawned a fashion style that became the essential wardrobe to accompany the music of the Sex Pistols and The Clash. Music and fashion closely adhered to the same do-it-yourself aesthetic and equally became destroyed, distressed and deconstructed. Clothing was purposely torn and ripped or distressed with razor blades and then crudely pieced back together with safety pins and chains. Slogans and bleach defaced the fabrics' original identity. These clothes yelled the same independence as punk music and deconstruction fully came of age.

Vivienne Westwood said at the time that 'I have a kind of in-built clock which always reacts against anything orthodox.'

The popularity of punk's radical look became so quickly co-opted and imitated through mass production that it ironically joined the same mainstream that its originators had fought against. High fashion was no slouch in responding to the trend and during the 1980s the Paris catwalks also used deconstruction in the collections of Jean Paul Gaultier, Yohji Yamamoto and Rei Kawakubo (b.1942).

Out on the street distressed clothing resurfaced during the 1990s when the 'Seattle Sound' exploded out of America and grunge was born. Like the Sex Pistols before them, bands like Nirvana and Pearl Jam adopted an anti-fashion dress code that complemented their individual rock sound. As part of their typically unkempt wardrobe, ripped jeans edged back into mainstream fashion. Subsequently, Marc Jacobs (b.1963) notoriously borrowed the grunge image of 'unfashion' for the Perry Ellis (1940–86) Spring 1993 collection, and although it earned him the accolade of 'guru of grunge' it also led to his dismissal from the company.

Above
Claire Billington
(2012)

Below
Rosa Ng (2011)

Opposite, right
Eleanor Mountfort
(2010)

Opposite, left
Rachel Lamb (2011)
In fashion design, erosion and re-assembly are useful means of testing the boundaries of accepted taste. Alexander McQueen said 'I find beauty in the grotesque. Like most artists, I have to force people to look at things.'

A further aspect of deconstruction not to be overlooked is the consequence of natural decomposition that happens over time. Rust, rot and natural decay create their own unique form of accidental art and organic graffiti. There is an infinite supply of inspirational beauty inherent in both urban and natural decay if you seek it out. The manner in which any two objects decay is never identical because the natural forces trigger different effects depending upon the local environment and conditions. Each individual object is capable of endowing its own particular attractiveness, and these conditions provide designers with a great opportunity for re-interpretation when directed towards fashion conclusions.

Hussein Chalayan has a history of monitoring the process of change and decay going back to his student days at Central Saint Martins School of Art. For his graduate collection in 1993, 'The Tangent Flows', he experimented by burying the garments in his back garden wrapped with corroded iron filings.

In the 20th century there is one fashion designer more than any other who has been linked with deconstruction and decay: Martin Margiela (b.1957). A graduate from the Antwerp's Royal Academy of Fine Arts, he became a design assistant at Jean Paul Gaultier for two years, before branching out on his own in 1988 with MMM (Maison Martin Margiela).

Margiela is the Banksy of the fashion world, preferring to remain virtually incognito. The personality of the designer has been removed at MMM and the focus is entirely upon his unique creations. Even the label on the clothes is an anonymous blank white rectangle with a circled identity number. A conceptual designer, he has always pushed against the boundaries of what constitutes contemporary fashion. Margiela has always been intrigued by the effects of weathering and decay on clothes. In 1997 he famously staged an exhibition of eighteen dressed mannequins in Rotterdam's Museum Boijmans Van Beuningen, in which each outfit was treated with differing strains of mould, yeast and bacteria that was allowed to gestate on to the clothes. He has also worked jewellry out of tinted ice cubes that streaked the clothes in blues and magenta as they melted. Deconstruction at MMM has resulted in literally turning garments inside out, with the hidden features of construction – shoulder pads, linings, raw seams – exposed as the focus for the style.

'Once upon a time … ': using a fashion concept

You have already become acquainted with the basic ingredients for a fashion sketchbook and how to source and expand your excavated research to test its viability as inspiration for contemporary fashion design. Now it is time to bind all these building blocks together to provide a visual identity or concept for your intentions. The concept represents the overriding narrative that establishes a focus for your ideas. Some designers use the concept as the initial kick-start to their designs, others allow a concept to emerge as their research and design process evolves. Either way it is crucial.

A concept in fashion provides the key to explaining the designs and is akin to a storyboard for a film director. It explains how all the disparate pieces of research join up to create something new, although not necessarily in a rigid, sequential order – rather it forms the circus marquee that rearranges its individually sourced performers for the eventual delight of its audience under a single, big-top attraction.

It will always be a very personal consideration by each designer. A concept will ensure that the research is developed into designs that are not misread. Sometimes the concept might be converted into the 'selling point' of the final collection, or it may remain a closely guarded secret that is only hinted at away from the studio and outside of the sketchbook.

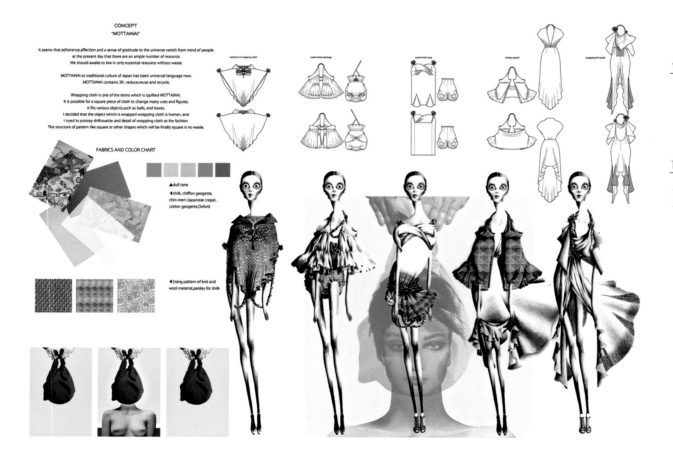

'I love designers who create a world that is inhabited by the characters that happen to wear their garments. A personal language; a work that doesn't go out of date. I'm talking about people like Margiela, Helmut Lang, Carol Christian Poell, Lee McQueen. These people have invented a universe of their own.'

Monika Bielskyte (b.1986)

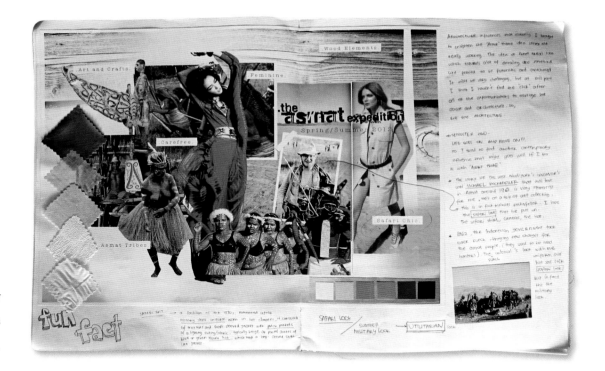

Right
Florestyn (2011)

Opposite
Yuka Kanagawa (2012)
A fashion concept should always be a personal response, whether you are working to a client's brief or researching your own private ideas. A concept enables you to express your individuality as a creative designer by directing the diverse ingredients of your research towards establishing a new fashion image.

Designers will often attach a title or name to their collection as a way of identifying their concept. This conveniently supplies an insider's guide to the designer's intentions and is usually exploited in the catwalk and press that accompanies the launch. Today, this branded approach to the presentation of fashion, usually as a spectacular visual entertainment that inflates the actual clothes using operatic gestures, is viewed as commonplace. Both Alexander McQueen and John Galliano (b.1960) embraced this *modus operandi* and fully exploited the potential of using a fashion concept to boost their latest collections beyond a runway of paraded clothes.

However, this technique of a collection concept in fashion is not as new as it might appear. Beginning in the late 1930s, the Italian maverick designer, Elsa Schiaparelli, had already pioneered these unorthodox techniques to direct interest away from her contemporaries and rivals. Her collections and salon fashion shows often used concepts and themes and were more theatrically staged than the usual couture shows using special backdrops and dramatic lighting. Unlike other Parisian couturiers, she was always concerned with the 'total' look of her creations and preferred to direct the entire ensemble, including designing the accompanying shoes, hats, gloves and jewellery as well as its styling and promotion.

Some examples of her thematic collections included metamorphosis manifested as the 'Butterflies Collection' (1937); a Botticelli-inspired 'Pagan Collection' (Autumn 1938); a geometric 'Astrological Collection' (Winter 1938/39); a harlequin patterned 'Commedia dell'arte Collection' (Spring 1939); 'Musical Instruments' (Autumn 1939) and most famously, the Dalí-collaborated 'Circus Collection' (Spring 1938).

Artists and designers have regularly taken their concept inspiration from a muse – either fictional or real – and work with this person in mind. One of the most celebrated examples from the last century is Andy Warhol and Edie Sedgwick (1943–71) in the 1960s. Within fashion, Jacques Fath worked with Bettina Graziani (b.1925); Yves Saint Laurent praised Catherine Deneuve (b.1943); Marc Jacobs has cited Sofia Coppola (b.1971); Halston (1932–90) credited Liza Minnelli (b.1946) and Tom Ford works with former editor-in-chief of French *Vogue*, Carine Roitfeld (b.1954), while Alexander McQueen and Philip Treacy (b.1967) both acknowledged Isabella Blow (1958–2007) as their muse. However, the most lasting fashion liaison has to be Hubert de Givenchy and Audrey Hepburn. It is impossible to sever the connections between the personal image of the actress and the timeless quality of the Givenchy house style.

For the duration of your sketchbook, the fashion concept acts like the cover-wrap that not only advertises the mood and theme of your designs, but will also weave the research together and cloak your ideas with their new and creative identity. It acts as a means of concentrating the design development within a single objective. It is possible to arrive at your creative concept from two contrasting points of view – a directly literal or narrative approach or via a more abstract or conceptual attitude. Both are equally as valid. It is down to personal taste and suitability.

One example of a narrative concept would be Vivienne Westwood's first London catwalk show in 1981. Following Malcolm McLaren's advice to 'look at history', Westwood researched 18th-century men's clothing at London's Victoria and Albert Museum, and engineered the androgynous collection that instantly became labelled the 'Pirate Collection', which marked the beginning of Westwood's involvement with her continuing trademark technique of the cut and heritage of historical tailoring. Her reinvented billowing sleeves and loose rectangular-cut shirts and trousers of highwaymen and dandies, spawned the short-lived 'New Romantic' image that was hastily adopted by British bands, such as Adam and the Ants, Duran Duran and Spandau Ballet. It was the individual way that Westwood brought the ingredients together that made the concept appear original and challenging.

Alternatively, you might decide to follow a more abstract methodology that allows you to expand upon current perceptions of fashion by employing a conceptual approach to organizing and directing your research. This is a non-literal representation because the subject isn't as easily identified in traditional fashion terms. Hussein Chalayan and Martin Margiela have often used this means of approach in their work; they both rely on highlighting the creative synergy between clothing and culture to question the value of contemporary fashion. They are not concerned with seasonal colours or falling hemlines – their rationale is to use a concept that asks questions rather than supplying a retail product.

In the 1980s the same attention to content rather than commerciality was the driving force behind the first generation of Japanese fashion designers to impact in the West. When Issey Miyake, Yohji Yamamoto, Rei Kawakubo and Junya Watanabe (b.1961) presented their innovative ideas at the prêt-à-porter exhibition in Paris, their radically conceptual approach was viewed as anti-aesthetic in approach. Their inventive cut and shaping and the disregard for colour unsettled the European fashion industry. Their intellectual artistry paved the way for the later wave of conceptual designers including Holland's Viktor (Horsting, b.1969) & Rolf (Snoeren, b.1969), Iris van Herpen (b.1984), Sara Vrugt (b.1981) and Belgium's Walter Van Beirendonck (b.1957), Dries Van Noten (b.1958), and Ann Demeulemeester (b.1959).

Above
Eleanor Mountfort (2010)
Centre
Rosa Ng (2011)

Below
Anna Larson (2010)
A fashion concept can be developed following either a narrative or abstract re-interpretation of your initial research.

The most popular way for a designer to flesh out their concept visually is with a mood or theme board. For presentation to a client a mood board would be prepared to a large format output or might be projected onto a screen. Within your sketchbook it will be scaled down in size but is no less important. Although the mood board has become much maligned in recent academic circles – mainly due to the ready acceptance of digital presentation – it still remains a vital piece of the overall jigsaw of your design ideas and needs to be given careful attention. It should never become a dumping ground to off-load visual research as a jumbled collage. It demands a considerable amount of creative flare and imagination to conjure up a suitably suggestive representation of your intentions. In outlining your concept it is important not to over-face the viewer with too many conflicting ideas.

In telling your story as a mood board you will need to give consideration to visualizing the facts in a creative and non-literal way. Thinking away from the obvious will provide a new insight to support your concept. Consider how advertising agencies inventively repackage the same product – whether it is cars or jeans – in order to seduce the buying public. By applying a radical concept to your own ideas you will similarly halt the uniformity of fashion.

It is best not to be over-reliant on secondary imagery for your mood boards. Downloads from the Internet have become easy prey, but they often have been uploaded in a low resolution that becomes pixilated when printed out at a large scale. Their easy access also lessens the exclusivity of your own mood board. And remember that tear sheets from the latest popular magazine won't necessarily give you the edge over a rival designer with the same access. Importing too many recognizable contemporary fashion images can easily swamp your own work. Whenever possible, try to employ your own photographs and self-generated artwork to ensure a more distinctive quality.

Left
Jade Elizabeth Hannam (2010/11)
A mood board should be able to draw all the disparate elements together and present them in an enticing and appealing manner without any confusion over what it represents.

The bigger picture: putting it into context

'Fashion does not exist in a vacuum. Fashion reflects culture; it reflects our times. A great fashion photograph can tell you just as much about what is going on in our world as any headline or TV report, so go out, go to the galleries, go to the theatre, read books, travel … all of that will come back to reward you later.'

Anna Wintour (b.1949)

Fashion in today's multicultural society is regarded as a dynamic, cultural and artistic undertaking. Nevertheless, it should never be viewed in isolation from the ever-changing world it occupies. Fashion will always be judged as a reflection of its time and culture. It has never been allowed to remain stagnant. The same time shifts that impact on society push fashion to constantly re-evaluate its purpose and importance. Fashion always functions in reaction to and as a reflection of the economic, political and cultural needs demanded by the society of the day. It may not necessarily always be apparent at the time, but in hindsight, the knock-on effects towards fashion and style are all too easy to appreciate.

You have already learned how juxtaposing diverse elements within your research can create new relationships to provide fresh opportunities for design direction. Another method for releasing the hidden potential within your findings is by cross-referencing the data with simultaneous worldwide events and developments. Whether through politics and warfare or social and ecological concerns, fashion designers have always absorbed the here and now into their clothes.

'Fashion is the image of an age and can tell its story better than speech.'

Karl Lagerfeld

Every fashion style or trend of the 20th century can be better appreciated by looking at the emerging economic and social climate that was prevalent at that time. It is often cited by economists that women's hemlines went up in times of prosperity (1920s and 1960s) and went down when times were bad (1930s and 1970s). It is important that you evidence in your sketchbook the research context to explain these swings in design and taste set against their immediate cultural backdrop. By digging beneath the surface gloss of fashion you are able to show the symbiotic relationship and significance of image and social change.

The creation of a timeline will widen the historical significance of your research and enhance its importance within the wider context of worldwide events. By understanding fashion's past, you will be in a better position to create its future. Overleaf is a timeline for the 20th century that pinpoints fashion's genealogy within the context of the cultural and historical events taking place during each decade.

Opposite
Kerrie Alexander (2012)
'Emasculated Status'
The context for this research was the widespread rioting across the UK during August 2011 and the unofficial uniform of the participants.

Above and centre
Felicity Baggett (2009)

Below
Lucy Taylor (2012)

WORLD OF ARTS	POPULAR CULTURE
1902: Gustav Klimt (1862–1918) paints the *Beethovenfries* **1902:** Louis Comfort Tiffany (1848–1933) opens the Tiffany Studios in New York **1905:** Expressionism is founded in Dresden by the group *Die Brücke* ('The Bridge') **1905:** Exhibitors at the *Salon d'Automne* in Paris dubbed *Les Fauves* ('The Wild Beasts') **1907:** Pablo Picasso's (1881–1973) *Les Demoiselles d'Avignon* introduces Cubism **1908:** Eight Realist painters known as The Ashcan School exhibit in New York **1909:** Sergei Diaghilev (1872–1929) establishes the *Ballets Russes* at the Paris Opera **1909:** Filippo Marinetti (1876–1944) publishes his 'Futurist Manifesto' in Paris	**1900s:** Scott Joplin's (1867–1917) syncopated ragtime begins a dance craze **1900:** The Kodak Brownie Camera is introduced by George Eastman **1902:** 'A Trip to the Moon' directed by Georges Méliès (1861–1938) opens in Paris **1902:** Teddy Bears are christened after Theodore Roosevelt (1858–1919) **1903:** William S. Harley and Arthur Davidson produce their first motorcycle **1903:** The first narrative motion picture, 'The Great Train Robbery' is directed and photographed by Edwin S. Porter (1870–1941) **1906:** Reginald A Fessenden (1866–1932) makes the first music radio broadcast **1907:** Louis Lumière (1864–1948) develops a process for colour photography **1908:** The Ford Motor Company assemble their first Model T automobile
1911: The founding of *Der Blaue Reiter* ('The Blue Rider') in Munich **1913:** Marcel Duchamp (1887–1968) creates kinetic sculpture 'Bicycle Wheel' **1913:** *The Rite of Spring* by Igor Stravinsky (1882–1971) premieres in Paris **1914:** Wyndham Lewis (1882–1957) and other artists launch Vorticism in England **1915:** Vladimir Tatlin (1885–1953) establishes Constructivism in Russia **1915:** Kazimir Malevich (1879–1935) pioneers Suprematism in Russia **1915:** Foundation of the Dada movement in Zurich **1917:** Marcel Duchamp (1887–1968) exhibits an upturned urinal in New York **1919:** Walter Gropius founds The Bauhaus School in Weimar	**1912:** German actress Henny Porten (1890–1960) emerges as the first film 'star' **1912:** Mack Sennett (1880–1960) creates The Keystone Studios to produce 'slapstick' films **1913:** The foxtrot is introduced at the Ziegfeld Follies in New York **1913:** The tango becomes a dance craze across Europe and the USA **1915:** David-Ward Griffith (1975–48) directs the epic film 'The Birth of a Nation' **1916:** A Brazilian recorded song '*Pelo Telefone*' introduces the 'samba' **1917:** The first commercial jazz recording 'Livery Stable Blues' is made in New Orleans **1919:** Robert Wiene (1880–1938) directs first expressionist film *The Cabinet of Dr Caligari*
1923: Arnold Schoenberg (1874–1951) introduces his 12-tone technique of 'serialism' **1924:** André Breton (1896–1966) issues his first 'Surrealist Manifesto' **1924:** George Gershwin's (1898–1937) 'Rhapsody in Blue' premieres in New York **1925:** *L'Exposition des Arts Décoratifs et Industriels Modernes* introduces Art Deco **1925:** The art exhibition *La Peinture Surréaliste* is held at Gallerie Pierre in Paris **1926:** Alexander Calder (1898–1976) creates his kinetic sculpture 'Cirque Calder' **1926:** Antoni Gaudí (1852–1926) dies leaving the Sagrada Família uncompleted **1929:** The Museum of Modern Art opens in New York	**1920:** Mamie Smith (1883–1946) makes the first vocal blues recording on Okeh Records **1922:** James Joyce (1882–1941) publishes *Ulysses* **1922:** The British Broadcasting Company (BBC) begins radio transmissions **1923:** The Cotton Club opens in Harlem, starring black-only entertainers **1923:** James P. Johnson's (1894–1955) musical 'Runnin' Wild' launches the Charleston **1925:** The *Revue Negre* in Paris introduces Josephine Baker (1906–75) **1926:** Fritz Lang (1890–1976) directs *Metropolis* **1927:** The first talking movie *The Jazz Singer* premieres in New York **1928:** Mickey Mouse makes his debut in Walt Disney's (1901–66) *Steamboat Willie* **1928:** Luis Buñuel (1900–83) co-directs *Un Chien Andalou* with Salvador Dalí (1904–89)
1932: Ansel Adams (1902–84), Imogen Cunningham (1883–1976) and Edward Weston (1886–1958) form Group f/64 in San Francisco dedicated to a 'pure' photography **1933:** Diego Rivera (1886–1957) creates a mural for New York's Rockefeller Center **1933:** Josef Albers (1888–1976) teaches at Black Mountain College, North Carolina **1936:** Max Bill publishes his manifesto '*Konkrete Gestaltung*' in Zurich **1937:** Salvador Dalí (1904–89) paints *Metamorphose de Narcisse* **1937:** Pablo Picasso's (1881–1973) *Guernica* is exhibited in Paris **1939:** Yves Tanguy (1900–55) paints 'Furniture of Time'	**1931:** EMI opens the largest recording studio in the world at Abbey Road in London **1931:** The 102-storey Empire State Building opens in New York **1933:** Ignacio Piñeiro's (1888–1969) release '*Échale Salsita*' introduces 'salsa' dance music **1936:** The Berlin Summer Olympics become a huge propaganda success for the Nazi Party **1936:** Charlie Chaplin (1889–1977) directs and stars in *Modern Times* **1938:** Volkswagen roll out their first Beetle automobile **1939:** The first appearance of the *Superman* comic strip **1939:** Bob Kane's (1915–98) *Batman* debuts as a daily comic strip **1939:** MGM release both *Gone with the Wind* and *The Wizard of Oz*
1940: Stone Age cave paintings discovered at Lascaux, France **1942:** Edward Hopper (1882–1967) paints *Nighthawks* **1942:** Albert Camus (1913–60) and Jean-Paul Sartre (1905–80) establish Existentialism **1944:** Francis Bacon (1909–92) paints 'Three Studies for Figures at the Base of a Crucifixion' **1945:** Jackson Pollock (1912–56) begins abstract expressionism with his 'splatter' paintings **1945:** Jean Dubuffet (1901–85) begins to collect 'Art Brut' **1947:** The Dead Sea Scrolls are discovered at Khirbet Qumran, Palestine **1947:** Henri Matisse (1869–1954) publishes his paper cut-out compositions *Jazz* **1948:** Pierre Schaeffer (1910–95) develops *musique concrète* **1948:** Karel Appel (1921–2006) forms the COBRA to pioneer abstract painting **1949:** George Orwell's (1903–50) novel *1984* is published **1949:** The premiere of *Death of a Salesman* by Arthur Miller (1915–2005)	**1940:** Peter Goldmark (1906–77) demonstrates the first colour television **1941:** Dizzy Gillespie (1917–93), Charlie Parker (1920–55), and Thelonious Monk (1917–82) introduce 'bebop' at Mintons's Playhouse in Harlem **1941:** Orson Welles (1915–85) directs *Citizen Kane* **1941:** 'El Rancho Vegas Hotel' becomes the first casino on the future Las Vegas Strip **1942:** The T-shirt as an outer garment is popularized by *Life* magazine **1945:** Roberto Rossellini's film (1906–77) '*Roma, città aperta*' inaugurates Neorealism **1946:** Muddy Waters (1915–83) records the first 'rhythm and blues' records for Chess Records **1947:** Aviator Kenneth Arnold (1915–84) makes the first US sighting of a UFO **1948:** Leo Fender (1909–91) invents the electric guitar **1949:** RCA Victor introduces the 7-inch 45 RPM vinyl record **1949:** Miles Davis' (1926–91) Nonet establishes 'cool jazz'

1900–1909

DESIGNERS	MILESTONE WORLD EVENTS
Gustav Beer (c.1875–c.1953) Madeleine Chéruit (d.1935) Georges Doeuillet (1865–1928) Jacques Doucet (1853–1929) Nicole Groult (1880–1940) Charles Klein (1867–1915) Paul Poiret (1879–1944) Caroline Reboux (1837–1927) Maison Redfern (est. London 1881) Charles Frederick Worth (1825–95)	**1900:** Sigmund Freud (1856–1939) publishes *The Interpretation of Dreams* **1901:** Queen Victoria (1819–1901) dies **1901:** Guglielmo Marconi (1874–1937) transmits the first telegraphic radio messages **1903:** Emmeline Pankhurst (1858–1928) forms the Women's Social and Political Union **1903:** The Wright brothers fly the first motorized airplane at Kitty Hawk, North Carolina **1905:** Albert Einstein (1879–1955) formulates the Theory of Relativity (E=mc2) **1906:** The San Francisco earthquake devastates the city **1906:** The Labour Party is formed in the UK **1909:** Louis Blériot (1872–1936) crosses the English Channel by airplane in 37 minutes

1910–1919

DESIGNERS	MILESTONE WORLD EVENTS
Jeanne Adele Bernard (1872–1962) Callot Soeurs (1895–1952) Baron Christoff von Drecoll (1851–1933) Lady Duff-Gordon (Lucile, 1863–1935) Mariano Fortuny (1871–1949) Jeanne Hallée (1880–1914) Herbert Luey (1860–1916) Maria Monaci-Gallenga (1880–1944) Jeanne Paquin (1869–1936) Ermenegildo Zegna (1892–1966)	**1912:** RMS *Titanic* sinks in the North Atlantic Ocean **1912:** Carl Jung (1875–1961) publishes *Psychology of the Unconscious* **1914:** The First World War breaks out in the Balkans **1914:** The USA and Panama open the Panama Canal **1916:** Margaret Higgins Sanger (1879–1966) opens the first birth control clinic **1917:** Vladimir Lenin (1870–1924) leads the Bolshevik Revolution in Russia **1918:** Spanish Flu pandemic breaks out resulting in 20 million deaths worldwide **1918:** The First World War ends **1919:** The IRA is formed in Ireland to fight for an independent Irish state **1919:** Afghanistan gains independence from Britain

1920–1929

DESIGNERS	MILESTONE WORLD EVENTS
Louise Boulanger (1806–67) Gabrielle 'Coco' Chanel (1883–1971) Sonia Delauney (1885–1979) Jeanne Lanvin (1867–1946) Salvatore Ferragamo (1898–1960) Lucien Lelong (1889–1958) Martial & Armand (1884–1960) Edward Molyneux (1891–1974) Lucile Paray (1863–1935) Jean Patou (1880–1936)	**1920:** The 18th Amendment to the US Constitution prohibits the sale of liquor **1920:** Mahatma Gandhi (1869–1948) founds the non-violent liberation movement in India **1920:** The 19th Amendment to the US Constitution grants women the right to vote **1922:** Leader of the Fascist Party, Benito Mussolini (1883–1945), seizes power in Italy **1922:** Vladimir Lenin creates the Soviet Union **1924:** Vladimir Lenin dies and Joseph Stalin (1879–1953) seizes power in the Soviet Union **1925:** Edwin Hubble (1889–1953) discovers the first galaxy outside the Milky Way **1927:** Charles A. Lindbergh (1902–74) flies non-stop from New York to Paris in 33.5 hours **1928:** Alexander Fleming (1881–1955) discovers penicillin **1929:** The US Stock markets crashes triggering the beginning of the Great Depression

1930–1939

DESIGNERS	MILESTONE WORLD EVENTS
Augusta Bernard (1886–1940) Alix 'Madame' Grès (1903–93) Jacques Heim (1899–1967) Mainbocher (1890–1976) Robert Piguet (1898–1953) Marcel Rochas (1902–55) Maggy Rouff (1896–1971) Elsa Schiaparelli (1890–1973) Victor Stiebel (1907–76) Madeleine Vionnet (1876–1975)	**1932:** Amelia Earhart (1897–1937) becomes the first woman to fly solo across the Atlantic **1932:** Sir Oswald Mosley (1896–1980) founds the British Union of Fascists **1933:** Leader of the Nazi party, Adolf Hitler (1889–1945), is appointed chancellor of Germany **1934:** Joseph Stalin begins the Great Purge of the Communist Party in the Soviet Union **1934:** Mao Tse-tung (1893–1976) leads the Long March of the Red Army in China **1936:** Edward VIII (1894–1972) abdicates the British throne to marry Wallis Simpson **1936:** Spanish Civil War breaks out between the socialists and Franco's nationalists **1938:** The Hindenburg airship catches fire while attempting to dock in New Jersey **1939:** The Second World War begins when German troops invade Poland

1940–1949

DESIGNERS	MILESTONE WORLD EVENTS
Marcelle Alix (1941–59) Jean Dessès (1904–70) Christian Dior (1905–57) Jacques Fath (1912–54) Germaine Lecomte (1889–1966) Madeleine de Rauch (1896–1985) Nina Ricci (1883–1970) Maggy Rouff (1896–1971) Pauline Trigère (1909–2002) Madeleine Vramant (active 1940s)	**1941:** Japan attacks Pearl Harbor in Hawaii and the USA enters the Second World War **1945:** The US drops two atomic bombs on Hiroshima and Nagasaki in Japan **1945:** The United Nations Organization is founded in New York **1945:** The Second World War ends **1946:** Sir Winston Churchill's (1874–1965) 'Iron Curtain' speech **1946:** The first non-military electronic computer (ENIAC) is built **1947:** India and Pakistan are partitioned and declared independent **1947:** The Jews are granted their own country in Palestine **1947:** Test pilot 'Chuck' Yeager (b.1923) breaks the sound barrier **1948:** Mahatma Gandhi (1869–1948) is assassinated by a Hindu extremist **1948:** The South African government establishes apartheid to segregate black from white **1949:** Mao Tse-tung wins a communist victory in China **1949:** NATO is formed by western European countries and the USA

WORLD OF ARTS	POPULAR CULTURE
1951: Lucian Freud (1922–2011) paints 'Interior at Paddington' for Festival Of Britain **1951:** Tachisme created as the European version of American Abstract Expressionism **1952:** Karlheinz Stockhausen (1928–2007) composes his first 'electronic music' **1952:** Harold Rosenberg (1906–78) coins the term 'action painting' **1956:** Richard Hamilton's (1922–2011) 'Just what is it that makes today's homes so different, so appealing?' is exhibited at London's Whitechapel Art Gallery **1958:** Yves Klein's (1928–62) empty exhibition 'Le Vide' pioneers 'conceptual art' **1959:** Allan Kaprow's (1927–2006) 'Eighteen Happenings in Six Parts' at the Reuben Gallery in New York introduces 'performance art'	**1953:** Ian Fleming (1908–64) publishes his first James Bond novel *Casino Royale* **1955:** The McDonald's franchise restaurant chain opens in Des Plaines, Illinois **1955:** Ray Charles' (1930–2004) 'I've Got a Woman' released **1955:** The first Disneyland opens in Anaheim, California **1955:** James Dean (1931–55) dies in a car crash on Route 466 near Cholame, California **1956:** 'Heartbreak Hotel' is Elvis Presley's (1935–77) first number one hit record **1958:** *The Tale of the White Serpent* becomes the first colour *anime* film from Toei Animation **1959:** Introduction of the Mini car designed by Alec Issigonis (1906–88) **1959:** Mattel, Inc. launch Barbie **1959:** The founding of Motown in Detroit with the release of The Miracles' 'Bad Girl'
1962: Andy Warhol's (1928–87) 'Marilyn Diptych' marks the arrival of Pop Art **1964:** Charles Csuri (b.1922) produces the first 'computer art' **1965:** Joseph Kosuth (b.1945) creates his installation 'One and Three Chairs' **1965:** Terry Riley's (b.1935) 'In C' introduces minimalist music **1965:** Vienna Actionism is founded to perform 'body art' **1966:** Carl Andre (b.1935) exhibits 'Equivalent (VIII)' **1967:** Darryl McCray (b.1954) aka 'Cornbread' creates 'graffiti art' in Philadelphia **1967:** Sol LeWitt (1928–2007) coins the phrase 'conceptual art' **1967:** Donald Judd (1928–94) exhibits 'Untitled (Stack)' **1968:** Louis K. Meisel (b.1942) founds the Photorealist art movement **1969:** The 'Art & Language' group established to promote 'conceptual art'	**1960:** 'Reggae' music emerges from Jamaica **1961:** Joseph Heller (1923–99) publishes *Catch-22* **1962:** Marilyn Monroe (1926–62) dies from a drugs overdose **1962:** *Spiderman* comic book by Stan Lee (b.1922) first appears **1962:** The Beatles first recording session at London's Abbey Road Studios **1965:** 'The Psychedelic Sounds of the 13th Floor Elevators' introduces 'psychedelic' music **1966:** England win the Football World Cup **1967:** The first Summer of Love is inaugurated at Haight-Ashbury, San Francisco **1967:** Velvet Underground, The Doors and Pink Floyd launch 'psychedelic rock' **1968:** Stanley Kubrick (1928–99) directs *2001: A Space Odyssey* **1969:** King Crimson, Pink Floyd and Yes create 'progressive rock' **1969:** Woodstock takes place at Max Yasgu's (1919–73) dairy farm, Bethel, New York
1970: Robert Smithson's (1938–73) 'Spiral Jetty' introduces Land Art **1971:** David Hockney (b.1937) paints 'Mr and Mrs Clark and Percy' **1972:** London's Tate Gallery acquires Carl Andre's (b.1935) 'Equivalent VIII' **1973:** Harold Cohen (b.1928) joins Stanford University's Artificial Intelligence Laboratory to develop the AARON software to simulate freehand drawing **1974:** The Terracotta Army unearthed at Xi'an in the Shaanxi province of China **1977:** Cindy Sherman (b.1954) begins her photographic series 'Untitled Film Stills' **1977:** George Coates (b.1936) establishes 'Performance Works' in Berkeley, California **1979:** Judy Chicago (b.1939) exhibits her installation *The Dinner Party*	**1970:** The first Gay Pride March in New York City commemorates The Stonewall Rebellion **1971:** Gloria Steinem (b.1934) founds the first feminist magazine *Ms Magazine* **1971:** Daisuke Inoue (b.1940) builds the first 'karaoke' machine in Kobe, Japan **1972:** 'Soul Makossa' by Manu Dibango (b.1933) introduces 'disco music' **1972:** Phillips introduce the first video-cassette recorder (VCR) **1973:** PBS' *An American Family* is the first 'reality show' on television **1974:** Ernő Rubik (b.1944) invents his cubed mechanical puzzle **1975:** The Sex Pistols launch first gig at St Martin's School of Art in London **1975:** Clive 'Hercules' Campbell (b.1955) pioneers 'hip hop' music **1977:** Elvis Presley's funeral takers place at Graceland, Memphis, Tennessee **1977:** George Lucas (b.1944) directs *Star Wars* **1978:** Toshihiro Nishikado (b.1944) releases 'Space Invaders'
1980: Georg Baselitz (b.1938) exhibits his first sculpture at the Venice Biennial **1980:** Jean-Michel Basquiat (1960–88) and Julian Schnabel (b.1951) begin to exhibit Neo-expressionist art in New York **1981:** Keith Haring's (1958–90) first exhibition at New York's Westbeth Painters Space **1981:** The first ARCO International Contemporary Art Fair is held in Madrid **1981:** The first exhibition of the 'Memphis Group' is held at the *Salone del Mobile*, Milan **1983:** Philippe Starck (b.1949) renovates the Palais de l'Élysée, Paris **1985:** Christo (b.1935) begins wrapping the Pont Neuf, Paris in polyamide fabric **1986:** Jeff Koons' (b.1955) casts his *Rabbit* sculpture in stainless steel **1989:** Censorship surrounds Robert Mapplethorpe's (1946–89) 'The Perfect Moment' exhibition at the Corcoran Gallery of Art, Washington DC	**1980s:** 'Breakdancing' becomes a dance craze **1980:** John Lennon (1940–80) is assassinated in New York by Mark Chapman (b.1955) **1980:** Arcade video game 'Pac-Man' is released in Japan **1981:** MTV begins broadcasting from New York City **1981:** Juan Atkins (b.1962) begins cutting 'techno' records in Detroit **1982:** Ridley Scott (b.1937) directs *Blade Runner* **1982:** The opening of the Haçienda nightclub in Manchester **1982:** Katsuhiro Otomo (b.1954) writes the cyberpunk manga *Akira* **1984:** Jesse Saunders' (b.1962) 'On & On' pioneers 'house' music **1984:** Guy Laliberté (b.1959) founds *Cirque du Soleil* in Baie-Saint-Paul, Quebec **1985:** 'Live Aid' at London's Wembley Stadium and J. F. K Stadium in Philadelphia
1992: Joseph Nechvatal's (b.1951) experiments result in 'The Computer Virus Project' **1994:** Vuk Ćosić (b.1966) and Alexi Shulgin (b.1963) found the 'net.art' movement **1994:** 30,000-year-old Chauvet-Pont-d'Arc Cave paintings found in southern France **1997:** Charles Saatchi's (b.1943) 'Sensation' exhibition at London's Royal Academy includes Damien Hirst (b.1965), Sarah Lucas (b.1962) and Tracey Emin (b.1963) **1998:** Guggenheim Museum stages retrospective of Robert Rauschenberg (1925–2008) **1999:** Camille Utterback's (b.1970) 'Text Rain' pioneers interactive digital art **1999:** Eduardo Kac (b.1962) creates his first 'transgenic' artwork 'Genesis'	**1991:** 'Grunge' music and fashion emerges out of Seattle, Washington **1991:** NWA's 'Efil4zaggin' becomes the first 'gangsta rap' album to top the Billboard charts **1993:** Sony Computer Entertainment launch their PlayStation in Japan **1993:** Marc Lowell Andreessen (b.1971) launches the first web browser Mosaic **1994:** Quentin Tarantino (b.1963) directs *Pulp Fiction* **1995:** John Lasseter's (b.1957) *Toy Story* is first computer-animated feature film **1996:** Toshiba launches the DVD in Japan **1997:** Gianni Versace (1946–97) is shot dead in Miami Beach, Florida **1999:** Shawn Fanning (b.1980) releases his Napster music-sharing platform **1999:** *Breitling Orbiter 3* makes the first non-stop balloon flight around the world

1950–1959		DESIGNERS	MILESTONE WORLD EVENTS
		Cristóbal Balenciaga (1895–1972) Pierre Balmain (1914–82) Hubert de Givenchy (b.1927) Norman Hartnell (1901–79) Charles James (1906–78) Herbert Kasper (b.1926) Anne Klein (1923–74) Claire McCardell (1905–58) Norman Norell (1900–72) Emilio Pucci (1914–92)	**1950:** The first successful organ transplant at Little Company of Mary Hospital, Illinois **1950:** The outbreak of the Korean War **1950:** US Senator Joseph McCarthy (1908–57) launches a 'witch hunt' against 'underground' communism **1951:** Carl Djerassi (b.1923) invents the birth-control pill at Syntex Laboratories in Mexico City **1952:** King George VI (1895–1952) dies and Princess Elizabeth (b.1926) becomes Queen at 25 **1953:** James Watson (b.1928) and Francis Crick (1916–2004) discover the structure of DNA **1954:** Roger Bannister (b.1929) runs the sub-four-minute mile in Oxford, UK **1955:** The Warsaw Pact is drawn up by eight communist states **1957:** The Soviet Union launches Sputnik 1, the first artificial satellite **1959:** Fidel Castro (b.1926) becomes Dictator of Cuba **1959:** Mary Leaky (1913–96) uncovers hominid fossil footprints in volcanic ash at Laetoli, Tanzania
1960–1969		Pierre Cardin (b.1922) André Courrèges (b.1923) Rudi Gernreich (1922–85) Barbara Hulanicki (b.1936) Jean Muir (1928–95) Mary Quant (b.1934) Paco Rabanne (b.1934) Yves Saint Laurent (1936–2008) Emanuel Ungaro (b.1933) Valentino (b.1932)	**1961:** Yuri Gagarin (1934–68) becomes first man in space **1961:** The communist government of East Germany erects the Berlin Wall **1961:** US involvement in the Vietnam War escalates **1962:** The Cuban Missile Crisis **1963:** Martin Luther King Jr (1929–68) delivers his 'I Have a Dream' speech in Washington **1963:** John F. Kennedy (1917–63) assassinated in Dallas, Texas **1965:** Malcolm X (1925–65) is assassinated in Manhattan's Audubon Ballroom **1966:** The Cultural Revolution in China is instigated by Mao Tse-tung **1967:** Christian Barnard (1922–2001) performs the world's first successful heart transplant **1969:** Neil Armstrong is the first man to walk on the Moon
1970–1979		Giorgio Armani (b.1934) Geoffrey Beene (1927–2004) Nino Cerruti (b.1930) Roy Halston Frowick (1932–90) Daniel Hechter (b.1938) Betsey Johnson (b.1942) Kenzo Takada (b.1939) Sonia Rykiel (b.1930) Gianni Versace (1946–97) Vivienne Westwood (b.1941)	**1970:** The Popular Front for the Liberation of Palestine hijack five aircraft bound for New York **1970:** Four students are killed by Ohio National Guardsmen at Kent State University **1971:** Robert Hunter (1941–2005) and other environmentalists found Greenpeace in Canada **1972:** The 'Watergate' scandal follows a break-in at the Democratic National Committee in Washington, DC **1973:** Motorola's Martin Cooper (b.1928) invents the first mobile wireless (cellular) phone **1975:** Ed Roberts' (1941–2010) Atari 8800 becomes the first personal computer **1976:** The first Concorde aircraft take off from London's Heathrow and Paris' Orly airports **1978:** Louise Joy Brown (b.1978) is the first baby born through human in-vitro fertilization (IVF) **1979:** Margaret Thatcher (b.1925) becomes the world's first female Prime Minister
1980–1989		Perry Ellis (1940–86) Jean Paul Gaultier (b.1952) Donna Karan (b.1948) Rei Kawakubo (b.1942) Calvin Klein (b.1942) Karl Lagerfeld (b.1933) Ralph Lauren (b.1939) Issey Miyake (b.1938) Thierry Mugler (b.1948) Yohji Yamamoto (b.1943)	**1980:** IBM introduce the first personal computer (PC) featuring an Intel 8088 microprocessor **1980:** The British SAS storm the Iranian Embassy in London to free 26 hostages **1981:** AIDS is first recognized by the US Centre for Disease Control and Prevention, Georgia **1981:** Lady Diana Spencer (1961–97) marries Prince Charles (b.1948) **1982:** Argentinian forces invade the Falkland Islands, prompting intervention by British forces **1984:** Apple debuts the Macintosh computer **1984:** Alec Jeffreys (b.1950) invents techniques for DNA fingerprinting and profiling **1986:** A nuclear accident takes place at the Nuclear Power Plant, Chernobyl, Ukraine **1987:** Beginning in Hong Kong, there is a worldwide stock market crash, 'Black Monday' **1989:** Protesting students are massacred by government troops in Tiananmen Square **1989:** The Berlin Wall is taken down
1990–1999		Walter Van Beirendonck (b.1957) Hussein Chalayan (b.1970) (Domenico) Dolce (b.1958) & (Stefano) Gabbana (b.1962) John Galliano (b.1960) Christian Lacroix (b.1951) Alexander McQueen (1969–2010) Martin Margiela (b.1957) Miuccia Prada (b.1949) Donatella Versace (b.1955) Junya Watanabe (b.1961)	**1990:** Nelson Mandela (b.1918) is freed from prison after 27 years **1990:** The invasion of Kuwait by Saddam Hussein's (1937–2006) forces leads to the first Gulf War **1991:** The Soviet Union is dissolved following President Gorbachev's (b.1931) resignation **1991:** The European Union sign the Maastricht Treaty to adopt the euro as their single currency **1993:** Terrorists explode a bomb beneath the World Trade Centre in New York **1994:** Apartheid ends in South Africa following the first free multiracial elections **1997:** Ian Wilmut (b.1944) successfully clones Dolly the sheep **1997:** Diana, Princess of Wales is killed in a car accident in Paris **1998:** Stem cells derived from a human embryo are isolated

Sketchbook task

'For something to be beautiful, it doesn't have to be pretty.'

Rei Kawakubo

Deconstruct/Reconstruct

Plato's saying that 'beauty lies in the eyes of the beholder' is always being tested in the world of fashion. Whether it is through the decomposition of the actual fabric or from the elimination of garment parts, designers are always fascinated by the challenges of flaunting convention and turning preconceptions inside out or upside-down (sometimes literally). As a fashion designer your ultimate consideration must always be the aesthetic appeal of your output despite all appearances to the contrary.

The tools for applying this incongruity are probably more accessible than you might think.

Although these practical techniques are as equally applicable in 3D as well as 2D, it is important that you always apply the same judgment over the inherent principles of design. Do not to fall into the trap of working in a hurry and without considering your actions. It is important that you appreciate that Deconstruct/Reconstruct is a creative process and not just a quick fix to a bad design. Even though the methods might appear crude the results can be surprisingly sophisticated.

1. Select a conventional fashion spread from a magazine and, using the techniques below, give it a creative makeover. Don't go for what you know will work – test out the unknown. Think carefully about how you want to deconstruct or remove and similarly what you want to add or enhance through reconstruction. Remember that joining fabrics together doesn't necessarily rely upon stitch any more than paper needs glue. Continually question your actions; for example, does everything need to slot perfectly together like a precisely cut jigsaw puzzle?

2. Add the results to your sketchbook – showing both before and after progression.

BASIC METHODS FOR DECONSTRUCTION		BASIC METHODS FOR RECONSTRUCTION	
Bleaching	Burning	Appliqué	Collage
Inverting	Melting	Gathering	Gluing
Ripping	Scratching	Patchwork	Pleating
Shredding	Slashing	Quilting	Stitching
Staining	Tearing	Tucking	Weaving

<u>Left and opposite</u>
Eugenia Alejos Garrido (2012)
'I love the concept of abstraction since no one knows its real meaning but everyone has their own idea of it. Each collage is made up of two things: to be well balanced and visually appealing. For me the tactility is very attractive. I like the feeling of the impossible and its opposite.'

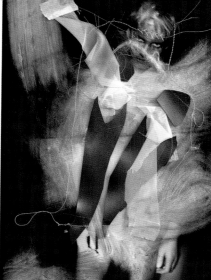

Sketchbook task

'To draw you must close your eyes and sing.'

Pablo Picasso

Blind contour: drawing without looking

A traditional warm-up exercise in art schools is the practice of drawing 'blind'. This doesn't involve wearing a blindfold but instead forces you to remain focused on the object you are drawing rather than continually shifting your gaze down to your paper and pencil. The drawing is usually done in a single continuous line without lifting the pencil away from the paper. It is common with this type of drawing to concentrate on the outer edges of an object rather than its compositional form and structure and to leave out any shading or tonal values.

Since you are prevented from seeing what you are actually drawing, blind contour drawing is an excellent way to train the eye to draw what it really sees rather than allowing the brain to auto-correct your actions and force you into drawing what you think you should be seeing instead.

For a fashion designer, blind contour drawing garment shapes is a great way to conjure up new and interesting silhouettes from existing garments.

1. Place a garment on a dress stand or get a friend to model it. Don't just look at it from its front angle; rotate the garment to get the most interesting contour.

2. It is probably best to work on a large sheet of paper – A2 upwards. Working on tracing paper is also a convenient way to transfer your outlines later. A useful starting point is to outline the garment in the air with your index finger. Then pick a point on the garment where your eye can track the contour of the garment. As your eye starts to move, so should your pencil. Remember, at no time should you look at your hand as it draws. An easy way to stop you peeping is to skewer your pencil through the middle of a paper plate and draw by holding your pencil underneath the paper plate. Try to complete the entire contour of the garment without lifting your pencil from the paper. Be generous with your drawing – a common mistake in blind contour is to make the drawing too small.

3. Repeat the exercise from different viewpoints and select those you feel have the most potential for translation.

4. Overlay your pre-selected shapes onto a sketched figure template (or photograph of a nude figure) to build up a series of interesting fashion contours. Increase the variations in garment shapes by rotating and flipping your blind contours prior to laying them over your figure.

5. Attach the results into your sketchbook for future development.

Above and opposite
Christabel Taylor (2010)
'In order to create initial shapes to adapt onto the body, I experimented by drawing blind with both my left and right hands. It was a really successful way to produce naive and almost crude garment contours.'

Showcase 3

Name:
Jessie Holmes
Nationality:
British
Graduate:
Ravensbourne Design
College, London, UK
Graduate Collection 2010:
'I Know Why the Caged
Bird Sings'

'Although I take my inspiration from lots of different things and I am constantly on the lookout for interesting objects and imagery, it is always the juxtaposition of the things I collect that really inspires me. I am interested in the way colours, images, textures and objects can complement or contrast with each other to create a particular mood or concept. For this particular project I took my inspiration from photos, money, stamps and objects that I had gathered on my personal travels. I also took inspiration from online blogs, books and magazines.

My sketchbook is very important to me; it is where I gather, explore and work through my ideas. I like to have an instant connection to my sketchbook and always work into an existing book. For this project I worked into my childhood atlas, giving my sketchbook a relevant and personal connection before I had even begun.

I pick out details, shapes, colours and textures from my research and make little sketches, embroideries and rough toile ideas. I begin to establish a colour palette and silhouettes from my research and will often layer imagery, drawings and fabrics in my sketchbook to build up my designs.

This project is about a caged bird who dreams of what lies beyond his bars. It's about freedom and achieving our hopes and dreams whatever our restrictions may be in life. To convey the beauty of freedom I looked to nomadic lifestyle and culture for rich colours, fabrics and detailed embroideries. I contrasted this with restricted cage shapes in areas of my silhouettes and within my tangled print designs.

My sketchbook has helped me record, research, develop and understand my thoughts. It is an illustration of the whole process from start to finish and I like to think I have created richer fashion designs because of my sketchbook.'

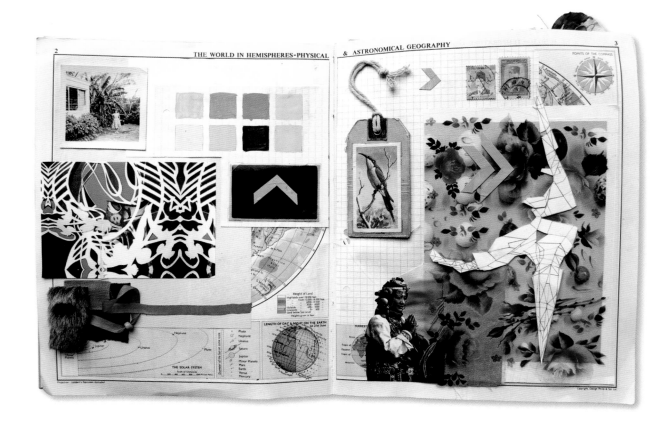

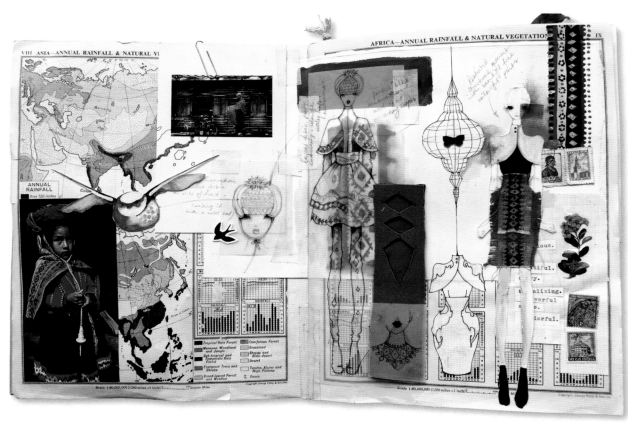

CHAPTER 4
Design direction: who, where and when?

'Design is not just what it looks like and feels like. Design is how it works.'

Steve Jobs (1955-2011)

The design direction stage is the final consideration before your research moves away from the information-gathering phase and starts to be reinterpreted and advanced into actual fashion designs.

Although fashion design is considered an artistic process, it is also an important player within the creative industries. Fashion today is deemed big business. There are more people involved globally in the designing, buying, selling and manufacture of clothes than in any other business. To an outsider fashion might be written off as just about frocks, shoes and handbags, but within today's business sector, fashion is unquestionably regarded as a key ingredient to the world's economy.

Left
Tiffany Baron (2012)
Understanding current market forces and evaluating your competitors is a necessary part of a designer's research and investigation.

According to a report commissioned by the British Fashion Council, the UK fashion industry directly contributed about $33 billion to the British economy in 2009. Boasting an industry with currently in excess of 816,000 employees, fashion is twice the size of the UK chemical or motor industries. The high regard for design within the fashion industry is not in dispute, but a designer must never overlook the fact that ultimately fashion is a commercial venture.

It is therefore important that your sketchbook shows that you are not only plugged into the contemporary fashion scene but are business savvy about the industry and the way it functions. You will need to evidence a series of key directional evaluations prior to embarking on the design development process. These will hone the focus of your designs by eliminating and weeding out the unnecessary and targeting your thoughts towards realistic and achievable objectives.

These considerations need to be in place before you can begin the transition to constructing your designs physically. Miss them out at your peril. Initially you will need to undertake a series of fact-finding missions to signpost your ideas and to understand the focus and validity of your ideas and design concepts:

- Which market sector are you aiming towards?
- Who is your target customer?
- Who are your competitors?
- What is the season?

Using this information, you will be able to confidently mix all your answers with your earlier research to begin the task of developing your designs.

The market sector

Fashion is usually pigeonholed into one of four basic category headings:

- Haute couture
- Ready-to-wear (prêt-à-porter)
- Mass market (mainstream fashion)
- Value fashion (cheap chic)

Every available fashion brand or label can be slotted into one of the above groupings. They classify the garment's price point and its intended target audience. All four are partial parasites that are easily recognized by their own individual qualities while benefiting from one another through both the trickle down and trickle up of prevailing trends and styles.

Haute couture (the crème de la crème of dressmaking)

'The difference between style and fashion is quality.'

Giorgio Armani

Haute couture is the smallest of the four categories and is respected as the summit of the fashion chain. Predictably, it is also the most expensive and exclusive of the fashion-market sectors. The term dates back to the 1850s when it was penned to describe the garments that Charles Frederick Worth manufactured at his salon in the Rue de la Paix, Paris. Contrary to the tradition of the times, clients visited Worth and not vice versa, and Worth's garments became the first to be sold under a designer's own name.

Since 1945, the accolade of haute couture has been protected by French law and only a handful of designers are allowed to trade as true couture houses. It is essential that they comply with the criteria laid down by the regulating body of the French fashion industry, the *Chambre syndicale de la haute couture* (Trade Union of Haute Couture).

Its associate rota comprises current members Chanel, Dior, Gaultier, and Givenchy plus former members Balmain, Lacroix, Rabanne and Saint Laurent. The *Chambre syndicale* also incorporates a separate category for foreign members that include Armani and Valentino.

It is worth noting that haute couture refers only to womenswear. There is no such thing as haute couture menswear. Part of the legislation is the requirement to produce bespoke custom-made clothes for specific clients that entail personal fittings. The couture house usually boasts two atelier workrooms; the *tailleur* responsible for daywear (coats, jackets and suits) and the *flou* given over to eveningwear and bridal.

Haute couture designers habitually exploit luxury fabrics to realize their creations and have a team of highly skilled in-house technicians to achieve the compulsory high quality of construction and finish. Each fashion atelier has also to showcase a new collection of no less than 35 pieces for both day and eveningwear twice a year. In addition, these catwalk shows are exploited as an opportunity to publicize all the other items that are sold under their branding including perfume, cosmetics and accessories.

Prices demanded for couture garments are prohibitive and cost many thousands of pounds. However, despite its obviously very wealthy clientele, haute couture is the least profitable of the four market sectors. Its one-time affluent Western patrons have recently been overtaken by new demands from China and the Middle East. For many, haute couture today preserves an image of the pinnacle of a craft that is admired from afar, but unattainable by the majority.

Right
Yuliya Bogdanova (2011)

Right
Clifford Faust (2011)

Above
Meagan Morrison (2011)
Haute couture has long been regarded as the apex of the fashion designer's skill and craft. It prides itself on its exclusivity and bespoke treatment of its clients. Haute couture remains the phoenix of the fashion market and despite all the couturier bankruptcy closures and business mergers, it continues to be respected for what it epitomizes: Karl Lagerfeld has said 'So long as the house of Chanel exists, couture exists.'

Ready-to-wear (prêt-à-porter)

'The finest clothing made is a person's skin, but, of course, society
demands something more than this.'

Mark Twain

Most couture houses also produce ready-to-wear or prêt-à-porter in addition to their couture
pieces. Distinct from haute couture, these designs are no longer intended as bespoke, one-off
pieces but use standardized sizing and are aimed towards a higher volume of distribution.
Along with haute couture, prêt-à-porter is also exhibited throughout the year. Unlike the
monopoly on haute couture fashion shows that take place in Paris, prêt-à-porter catwalks are
now staged in all the major fashion capitals around the world – London, New York and Milan –
although usually in advance of haute couture. This second tier in the fashion-market hierarchy
is directed towards a wider consumer base than couture. The intention behind prêt-à-porter is
to provide designer level clothing that maintains the superior fabrics and workmanship found
in couture. Garments still demand a relatively high price but now in the region of hundreds
rather than thousands of pounds. They are produced under strict adherence to quality control
specifications and are then distributed in exclusive designer shops and small independent
outlets, usually as limited editions.

Even with its lower price point, prêt-à-porter returns a better profit turnover than couture
due to its increased volume output and wider availability of garments.

This page
Eugene Czarneck (2012)
Three sketches of
designer label clothes.

Above
Sreejith Sreekumar
(2011)
Sartorial elegance
in a formal menswear
line-up for Italian
label, Ermenegildo
Zegna, who distribute
their collections
across 86 countries
throughout the world.

Although the origins of ready-to-wear date from the aftermath of the Second World War, when affordable off-the-peg lines were first filtered down by the majority of French couture houses and paper patterns were being licensed for reproduction in Italy and the USA, the term remains synonymous with Yves Saint Laurent who put prêt-à-porter firmly on the global fashion map.

He was the first French couturier to jump ship and simultaneously distribute his own ready-to-wear line. The first Rive Gauche outlet opened at 21 rue de Tournon, Paris on 26 September 1966. By tapping into the accelerating pace of fashion,

Saint Laurent upped the tempo and turnaround of his fashion line (now showing four times a year) to the extent that Rive Gauche pulled in more profit than his haute couture collections. The co-founder of St Laurent's couture house Pierre Bergé (b.1930) said, 'By opening a boutique separate from his fashion house, Saint Laurent was actually performing a revolutionary act, moving away from aesthetics into the social arena. It was a manifesto.' This diffusion of designer labels has since included D&G (Dolce & Gabbana); Mui Mui (Prada); Polo (Ralph Lauren); Jeans Jungle (Kenzo) and DKNY (Donna Karan).

Mass market (mainstream fashion)

'One week he's in polka dots, the next week he's in stripes.
'Cos he's a dedicated follower of fashion.'

Song lyric 'Dedicated Follower of Fashion' (1966),
Ray Davies (b.1944)

In complete contrast to haute couture and prêt-à-porter, mass fashion sets out to support the demands of a mainstream fashion audience. Exclusivity is replaced by popularity. It is the area that provides the majority of the world's dress codes. Mainstream fashion has become very good at appropriating the latest designer trends – either moving up from the street or trickling down from designer level – and adapting them for mass consumption.

New fashion styles can appear in the retail outlets and chain stores very quickly, which has given rise to the term 'fast fashion'. Fast fashion does not adhere to the bi-annual catwalk shows to reveal its new trends. Availability of the product moves fashion away from a designer's dictates and places the final image choice in the hands of the consumer.

The turnover is usually very swift and stock is continually updated. In the case of Spanish retail giant, Zara, new deliveries are maintained weekly to guarantee customer choice. It is vital that the supply chain in fast fashion is highly efficient and flexible so that it can react quickly to changes in consumer demand.

Obviously there is none of the labour-intensive couture atelier approach, with the majority of the merchandise manufactured in Asia and Eastern Europe. Fabrication and trimmings cannot be as expensive to meet the value-for-money approach at the checkout.

Key marketing strategies, more so than with couture or prêt-à-porter, are vital for the economy of mass fashion. Unlike couture's garments, mass fashion is sold as disposable fashion that will quickly go out of date, but is offered at a low enough retail price point to generate further purchases.

Mainstream has often been regarded as the poor relation in the fashion stakes. Without a named designer heading each brand, retailers within mass fashion began buying into the exclusivity market by commissioning designer ranges and celebrity collaborations to appear alongside their usual store merchandise. Initially this was usually an incognito relationship (Paul Smith (b.1946), Betty Jackson (b.1949) and Katharine Hamnett (b.1947) all worked behind the scenes at M&S), but it has now become a competitive marketing strategy in mass fashion to flaunt designer and celebrity status within the retail environment. UK department store Debenhams plays host to a long list of accomplished designer names, including Ben de Lisi (b.1955), John Rocha (b.1953), Matthew Williamson (b.1971) and Jonathan Saunders (b.1977), while Topshop generated big headlines with its celebrity collaboration with Kate Moss.

'I'm not a designer. I've never been to school or been trained. I can't draw a dress, really. But I know what I like.'

Kate Moss (b.1974)

H&M, who have similarly exploited the celebrity bandwagon, have also offered regular limited-edition collections including collaborations with Karl Lagerfeld, Stella McCartney (b. 1971), Jimmy Choo, Sonia Rykiel (b.1930) and Donatella Versace (b.1955) while Alexander McQueen produced a fashion line for the US chain store, Target, and Giles Deacon worked on ranges for New Look in the UK.

Street fashion is often erroneously bundled together with mass fashion. However this urban style is outside the remit of any designer or retailer to control since it is all about the originality that each wearer brings through their personal ability to apply style and design to their own wardrobe and appearance. It is an important feeder for all four strands of the fashion market. Many trends are pioneered out on the street and today the latest looks are instantly broadcast through the plethora of fashion blogs and social media sites. Street fashion is primarily associated with the image of youth and sub-culture and has spawned some of the most iconic imagery of the last century: teddy boys, punks, goths and hip-hop.

Opposite
Carla Williams (2012)
Instantly relatable fashion trends that guarantee quick turnovers are the staple requisite of the mass-market retail sector.

Above
Hollie Louise Newton (2012)
Mainstream fashion retailers sustain their high-street identity by engaging with a multitude of diverse marketing strategies.

Below
Paul Kim (2012)

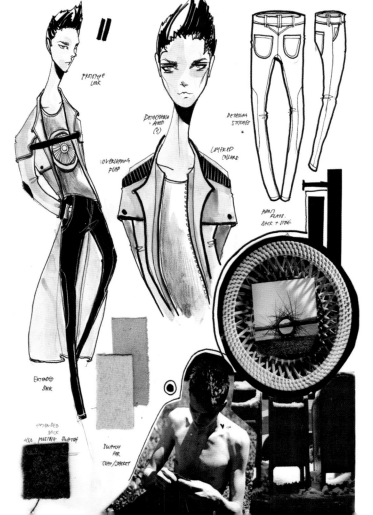

Value fashion (cheap chic)

'Never use the word 'cheap'. Today everybody can look chic in inexpensive clothes (the rich buy them too). There is good clothing design on every level today. You can be the chicest thing in the world in a T-shirt and jeans – it's up to you.'

Karl Lagerfeld

At the lower end of the market chain – and for most fashionistas of the time, certainly off the fashion radar – was the introduction of clothing within supermarkets. Suddenly you could buy a new T-shirt while you were doing the weekly food shopping. With its emphasis on 'stack 'em high, sell 'em cheap', the garments are mass-produced in popular sizes at very high volume, to keep the prices within a shopper's budget. Founder of the high street label NEXT George Davis, pioneered his George at ASDA range in 1990, in an attempt to bring a fashion stamp of approval to the supermarket's merchandise. Current George brand director, Fiona Lambert, said 'It is fast fashion, but only in the sense that we're making it quick to find.'

Other UK supermarkets took longer to jump on to the branding bandwagon – Tesco in 2002 and Sainsbury's in 2004 – but they both shocked the industry by their knock-down prices using quality fabrics: 100% cashmere coats went on sale at Florence & Fred (Tesco) for under £60, and the Tu range at Sainsbury's included cashmere sweaters at £15. However, the decreasing price point started to work against the value appeal, with accusations of exploitation in the CMT (cut-make-trim) supply chain rife in the media. Ethical fashion and charity work have done much in recent years to improve the image throughout the sector to the extent that UK outlet, Peacocks, now proudly brands itself as 'the leading value fashion retailer'. Richard Kirk, Peacocks chief executive, said 'Peacocks has changed from being a value business to a discount fashion brand. We're now a fashion business.'

Left Sponsorship is an effective way for supermarkets to sidestep their fruit and veg reputation and to pull down some fashion kudos instead. George at ASDA sponsor the annual Graduate Fashion Week exhibition that provides a platform for fashion colleges to promote their students out into industry. Bath Spa University graduate, Chloe Jones (left) was awarded the George Gold Award at the 2012 Gala Catwalk Show – previous recipients have included Stella McCartney, Giles Deacon and Matthew Williamson. (Photography Carolina Turner (above), Jack Grange (below).)

Away from the supermarket environment, value fashion had already made an appearance on the high street as far back as 1969, when Irish-based company Primark opened its first outlet in Dublin. Currently filling over 230 stores (now including Germany, Belgium, Austria and the Netherlands as well as the UK), its focus is on catching the imagination (and pocket) of a young demographic with a throwaway attitude to fashion. It has spawned similar companies across Europe: Kiabi in France, Takko Fashion in Italy and Mango in Spain.

Below
Hollie Louise Newton (2012)
Annotated shop report on UK High Street value trader Primark.

The store windows display the popular fashion trends of the moment, modelled on simple white mannequins, with a seasonal theme to the trend. Outfits are styled within comfortable fashion boundaries. In store and window graphics are plain, with lots of colour blocks used to section the differnt areas of the store. A rushed store environment is portrayed with fast fashion at hand. The models used within the posters are unique to their fashion face.

Target customer

'This is the most important question a designer can ask themselves, because these days, there's no room in the market for just another collection or just making clothes. To have any chance of becoming relevant you need to find your customer and speak to her in a consistent and meaningful way.'

Shira Sue Carmi (b.1977)

Each of the previous four fashion bandings is discernible by its own specific customer profile. To move your design ideas towards a conclusion you will need to identify your own intended target customer. These are the people that will eventually buy and wear your designs, so it is critical to know all about them. Establishing a customer profile will feed back into your design development process, and help to make your designs viable in today's highly competitive fashion marketplace. It is all about matching your own creative abilities with the sector of the market that will eventually want to purchase your designs.

Don't be afraid to use yourself as a guide. Donna Karan (b.1948), established her interchangeable 'Seven Easy Pieces' essential ranges based purely upon her own requirements as a professional career woman in the 1980s, bored with wearing the traditional power suit day in, day out.

It is crucial to be detailed in your customer profiling. You will need to compile a full list of characteristics that define your intended customer. Start by working your way through the broader demographics of gender, age, income and social groupings, to more specific lifestyle traits like personal values and aspirations, to fully flesh out your customer. By understanding not only what they wear but also what motivates them to select certain clothes you will establish a connection that will feed directly into your design development. If their choice was merely one of necessity, then a throw-over blanket might suffice. However, one of the basic rules of marketing is that consumers buy because of want and not necessarily need. The question you need to be asking is, what type of blanket would it be – fabric, colour, plain or patterned? A customer profile should provide you with these answers.

Several of the high street groups are now in the habit of christening their fictional target customers by name to make them even more real to the design team.

One of the easiest methods of identifying your own target market is to look within an existing customer base. Who buys which label? Why do they shop within certain stores? What have they got in common as a group? By analyzing your target customer demographic you will begin to understand the person behind the facts.

There are various ways to approach establishing a customer profile. Some designers prefer to prepare a written narrative around their intended customer – like a playwright establishing a character. It is also valid to build up a visual customer profile through a collage assembly. Whichever method you decide to employ in your sketchbook, it is important that you consider both quantitative (age, income, etc.) and qualitative (occupation, personality, etc.) data. The following headings will assist you in segmenting a target market and building up a customer profile. Always remember that the best research unsurprisingly comes from primary sources — in other words, you should collect the information first hand or use real-life situations when possible.

Demographics:
Gender * Age * Nationality * Income * Education * Occupation

Geographics:
Regional location * Climate

Psychographics:
Personality * Attitudes and values * Lifestyle * Interests

Behaviours:
Social class * Level of knowledge *
Brand-loyalty characteristics * Appreciation of quality

Opposite
Rachel Lamb (2009)
A customer profile needs to summarize the identity of the consumer by looking at lifestyle as well as fashion.

Above
Hollie Louise Newton (2012)
Compiling comparative British high street customer profiles is a way of understanding the needs and habits of the buying public.

Shop report

'It's always the badly dressed people who are the most interesting.'

Jean Paul Gaultier

Now that you have defined your market sector and typical customer, it is essential to take stock of what is already out there, and who your competitors in the future might be. Retail research is a very inexpensive but a valuable form of understanding fashion design. It is fundamental for any fashion designer to be plugged into the contemporary fashion retail scene.

Visiting fashion outlets and comparing competing stores is extremely informative. You will not only have the opportunity to see the merchandise on offer but can also check to see which are the movers, and which garments are staying on the racks. At first glance, it might appear off-putting that all tastes and styles already appear to be provided for. But closer inspection might present gaps in the market for a niche approach to a design sector that is not readily available, or the potential for a reinvention of a style that is presently off the radar.

The mass-market sector regularly carries out comparative shop reports in order to keep abreast of its competitors and to spot overlooked opportunities for development. It is not only important to recognize which colours or fabrics attract customers, but also to look at the branding and price points that secure sales. To the trained eye it is also possible to spot the evolution of an upcoming direction or trend from a comparative shop report. This type of information acts as a guide to when to launch a new style or introduce alternate fabrications. Most of the forecasting and prediction agencies listed in Chapter 2 pay a great deal of attention to the retail high street and call upon a body of international style scouts to check developments and report on the changes in the major fashion capitals across the world.

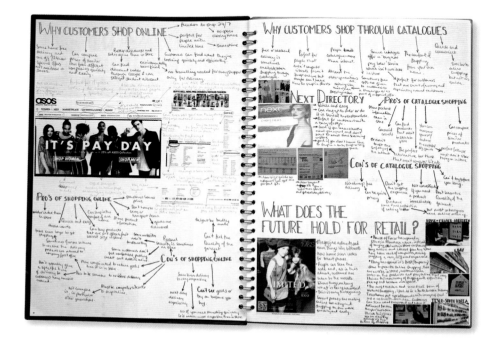

Left
Anna Larson (2011)

Opposite
Hollie Louise Newton (2012)
You will need to be focused and critical in your evaluation of the facts. Becoming visually objective is sometimes difficult in fashion but a necessary trait when compiling a shop report.

Department stores: large choice of buyer-selected fashion available under one roof (Saks of Fifth Avenue, Bloomingdales, New York; Harrods, London; Galeries Lafayette, Paris).
Independent designer shops (boutiques): specialist selection of ready-to-wear designer fashion (Browns of South Molton Street, London; Colette, Merci, L'Eclaireur Sévigné, Paris; 10 Corso Como, Milan; Jane Davidson/Pam Jenkins, Edinburgh; Soto, Berlin; Odin, New York).
Multiples: a chain of scattered high street chain stores operating under a parent company (Jigsaw, Topshop, French Connection, Gap).
Concessions: a rented shop space within a department store for smaller independent-label use.
Franchises: a retail distribution of shops managed locally but under a parent group heading (MEXX, Saint Tropez Clothing, Rohan, Benetton, Etam, Esprit).
Discount/Off-price stores: discontinued lines from all levels of the market (TK Maxx, Loehmann's, Winners, Toronto Canada, Burlington, Boston, Marshalls).
Factory shops and retail-outlet villages: manufacturers offering overstocked, ends of lines or damaged merchandise direct to the customer at a knock-down price (Fashion Outlets of Niagara Falls; Le Marche, Italy; DFO, Melbourne).
Street markets: similar to discount stores, but more transient and often trading in seconds at bargain prices (Petticoat Lane, London; Chiang Mai, Thailand; The Souks, Marrakesh).
Alternative markets: a mix of vintage and second-hand goods with young entrepreneurs testing out their designs (Camden Lock, Portobello Road, London; Le Marché aux Puces St-Ouen, Paris; Bondi Beach, Sydney; Die Nolle, Berlin).
Shopping centres/malls: vast retail complexes, usually sited away from a city, with the convenience of multiple merchandisers gathered in one place (South China Mall, Dongguan; SM City North EDSA, Philippines; West Edmonton Mall, Alberta).
Mail order: historically very popular disseminator of fashion usually photographed in intentionally aspirational locations (Boden, Littlewoods, Freemans, La Redoute).
Internet: a 24/7 approach to retail with a growing body of pureplay fashion retailers (ASOS, Net-a-porter, Koodos, The Outnet).
Pop-up shops/guerilla stores: a temporary outlet usually appearing unannounced overnight with a 'buy it while you see it' approach (Vacant, Designer's Emerge, Comme des Garcons, Nike).

There are varying levels of retail outlets for fashion, ranging from value retailers such as high-volume Primark and Walmart, to luxury designer boutiques like Louis Vuitton, Prada and Hermès, who aim to attract a more discerning clientele by their award-winning flagship emporiums. As expected, high street chains and shops dominate the global fashion market. Yell.com currently identifies more than 12,000 women's fashion retailers in the UK alone. Opposite is a list of the main fashion retail environments.

When carrying out your own shop report and analysis it is important to consider the total retail experience and not just the garments themselves:

- Location and proximity to other shops
- Window displays, branding and visual merchandising
- In-store atmosphere
- Key concepts on offer
- Quantities per style and sizing
- Use of colour, fabric and cut
- Trimmings and detailing
- Production values: country of origin/finish/etc.
- Price points.

A minimalist window display presents the re-occurring logo 'I am...' which can be seen across many seasons of their work. A wave of white washes over their current sleek store environment which supports the 'expensive' look and feel of the store. The focus is centred on their high-class clothing modelled by faceless white mannequins. High security is set in place to ensure the standards of the store and changing rooms retain the styling within the store. 'Chic' models are used on in store graphics in addition to in their magazines which are readily available in store and throughout their campaigns.

BRAND PROFILE

The fashion calendar: knowing when and where

Having identified your market, customer and competitors, there is one final consideration before bringing all your design ingredients together in your sketchbook – which season are your clothes aimed at? This is a fundamental consideration within fashion design and cannot be disregarded or taken as read. A designer that designs in a time vacuum is instantly disadvantaged. There is little point presenting garments for a summer season if all the attention of the media and the buyers' focus is on winter. Everything in the fashion industry is governed by the seasonal displays of new collections.

> 'It's always about timing. If it's too soon, no one understands. If it's too late, everyone's forgotten.'
>
> Anna Wintour

New York was the first city to host a fashion week in 1943. France had previously held the world's monopoly on premiering the latest trends and styles but was then in the midst of the Nazi occupation and the regular Paris fashion shows were cancelled. The opportunity for a change of focus was seized upon by US fashion publicist, Eleanor Lambert (1903–2003), who staged the first New York Fashion Week (at the time christened 'Press Week'), consisting of 53 American designers, at the Plaza Hotel in New York. This was the catalyst that prompted the establishment of the 'Big Four' as the foremost global venues in which to catch the latest fashions – New York, London, Milan and Paris. Each city designated a week's calendar slot every six months to allow designers to showcase their latest ideas in advance of the approaching seasons. Today's fashion industry has long outgrown any such geographical restrictions and cities across the world now also play host to the hottest trends through their own alternative fashion events.

Fashion weeks are always scheduled in the same order (see opposite). The fashion cycle is always anchored around the spring/summer collections (first exhibited the previous autumn) and the autumn/winter collections (exhibited earlier in spring).

The need for exhibiting several months in advance of the intended season is to allow interest by the media and buyers to generate adequate advance orders from retailers. This in turn will ensure that shops have sufficient stocks available and that there is ample matching press coverage prior to the launch of the actual season's fashion designs. It is imperative that everything is clearly signalled and adhered to and that designers and industry work hand-in-glove to guarantee the success of all parties.

The collections scheduled for January and July sometimes include a pre-collection to allow buyers and loyal regulars a sneak-peek preview to herald in the season's new looks. Larger fashion houses will also probably produce a more commercial range of clothes intended towards off-the-rack sales rather than the press-coverage objective of the catwalk shows. Slotted between the two primary fashion weeks there are also smaller capsule collections that are aimed at the Christmas and summer vacation retailing periods. Available in store before the arrival of the spring ranges, the pre-Christmas deliveries offer holiday and cocktail wear (often known as the 'cruise collection'), followed closely by the high-summer fashion lines that include resort and swimwear.

High-street retail chains still operate within the fashion calendar but phase in different concepts throughout each season. This drip-feed system allows retailers to employ a cascading approach by disseminating new trends across a sustained period rather than releasing everything up front and it creates the impression of always having something new to offer to the consumer.

As well as the wholesale fashion shows that introduce the new season's collections each year, there are major trade fairs around the world that showcase the future yarn and fabric trends. These are usually timed at six months prior to the runway shows to enable designers to buy into the new predictions.

WOMENSWEAR	FUTURE SEASON	
EVENT	Autumn/Winter	Spring/Summer
São Paulo Fashion Week, Brazil	Mid-January	Mid-June
Hong Kong Fashion Week, Hong Kong	Mid-January	Early July
Mercedes-Benz Berlin Fashion Week, Germany	Mid-January	Early July
Bread & Butter, Berlin, Germany	Mid-January	Early July
Modea Paris Haute Couture, France	Late January	Early July
AltaRomAltaModa (Rome Fashion Week), Italy	Late January	Early July
Amsterdam International Fashion Week, Netherlands	Late January	Mid-July
Bangalore Fashion Week, India	Early February	Late July
Copenhagen Fashion Week, Denmark	Early February	Early August
Stockholm Fashion Week, Sweden	Early February	Mid-August
Mercedes Benz Fashion Week Madrid, Spain	Early February	Early September
Istanbul Fashion Week, Turkey	Early February	Early September
Munich Fashion Week, Germany	Mid-February	Mid-August
Mercedes-Benz Fashion Week New York, USA	Mid-February	Mid-September
Couture Fashion Week, New York, USA	Mid-February	Mid-September
London Fashion Week, UK	Mid-February	Mid-September
Milan Women's Wear (Moda Donna), Italy	Late February	Late September
Modea Paris Ready-to-wear, France	Late February	Late September
Mercedes-Benz Fashion Week Johannesburg, South Africa	Early March	Late October
Tokyo Fashion Week, Japan	Mid-March	Mid-October
Mercedes-Benz Fashion Mexico, Mexico	Late March	September/October
Beijing Fashion Week, China	Late March	Late October
Volvo Fashion Week, Moscow, Russia	Early April	Mid-October
Shanghai Fashion Week, China	17-23 April	Autumn/winter
Dubai Fashion Week, United Arab Emirates	Mid-April 2011	Mid-October

MENSWEAR	FUTURE SEASON	
EVENT	Autumn/Winter	Spring/Summer
Pitti Immagine Uomo, Florence, Italy	Mid-January	Late June
Milano Moda Uomo, Milan, Italy	Mid-January	Late June
Mode à Paris: Men's Fashion, France	Mid-January	Late June
Mercedes-Benz Fashion Week Madrid: Menswear, Spain	Early February	Early September
Mercedes-Benz Fashion Week New York, USA	Mid-February	Mid-September

SPECIALIST MARKETS	
Childrenswear: Pitti Immagine Bimbo, Florence, Italy	Late January and late June
Bridal: Bridal Fashion Week, New York, USA Barcelona Bridal Week, Spain	Mid-February and early May
Swimwear: Rio de Janeiro Fashion Week São Paulo Fashion Week, Brazil	Late May and Mid-June
Footwear: Expo Riva Schuh Riva del Garda, Italy GDS, Düsseldorf, Germany	June, March and September
Ethical Fashion Shows: Berlin, Paris	Early July and Early September

YARN AND FABRIC FAIRS	
Pitti Immagine Filati, Florence, Italy	Late January and early July
Moda In, Milan, Italy	Early February and early September
Première Vision, Paris, France	Mid-February and mid-September
Expofil, Paris, France	Mid-February and mid-September
Prato Expo, Milan, Italy	Mid-February and mid-September
Interstoff Asia Essential, Hong Kong	Mid-March and early October
Yarn Expo, Beijing, China	Late March
Yarn Expo, Shanghai, China	Mid-October

Sketchbook task

Nature knows best: harvesting your own seasonal colour palette

Working out an appropriate colour palette each season is usually the starting point for establishing your intended design direction. Colour forecasters will have already drawn up their own predictions for the forthcoming season, but you can also build your own colour palette using this digital shortcut approach that relies upon nature to ensure a harmonious palette. By using a representative outdoor scene you can be confident that the natural colours will blend and work together and provide you with an appropriately atmospheric seasonal colour scheme. After sampling colours from the image you will be able to archive your selection as a customized swatch set to use as a directional guide to support any future design-development activity.

1. Open up your selected photographic image in Adobe Photoshop. You can either work from your own photograph or use an Internet-sourced image.

2. Now open up the Swatches Palette (Window > Swatches) and delete all the current colours. This needs to be done one colour at a time, but a quick way is to hold down your Option (Mac)/Alt (Windows) key as you hover the cursor over the colour block in the top left corner. The normal cursor will revert to a scissors icon and by clicking on the colour swatch it will be deleted. Continue clicking over the same spot to remove all the current colour blocks.

3. Return to your photographic image and filter the image into a generous mosaic pattern (Filter > Pixelate > Mosaic). Adjust the filter to provide about 25 mosaic tiles down the longer of the image's sides. You will now have a pixilated representation of your seasonal image. Select a series of about 6–8 connected colour tiles (in a line or rectangle). There will usually be a variety of inspirational choices ranging from closely related colours towards more contrasted combinations. You should take time to decide which work best for you. Make sure there are no duplications. When you are happy with your selection, mark a box around them for easy identification (Rectangular Marquee Tool > Edit > Stroke). In the drop-down menu select a contrasting colour to your palette choice with a width of around 5 pixels.

4. So that you can easily access your palette, you will need to store the colours individually as a new swatch set. Using the Eyedropper Tool select each of your pre-selected mosaic blocks in turn and click on the New Swatch icon at the base of the Swatches window to load the colours into your new swatch set.

5. After storing all of your colours you will need to save your seasonal palette for future reference by clicking the arrow in the top-right corner of the Swatches window to reveal the drop down menu and selecting 'Save Swatches' into the Colour Swatches folder (usually default). At the dialog box prompt enter a suitable name and click 'Save'. To return to your original default colour swatches, click the same arrow and select 'Reset Swatches'.

6. To call up your seasonal palette all you need to do is open the Swatches window, click on the arrow in the top right corner and select 'Replace Swatches' as your option.

Sketchbook task

'Say it with fashion': creating on-trend alphabets

Being on trend can be an exhausting (and sometimes expensive) treadmill that makes inroads into daily life through its initial launch on designer catwalks, emulation in magazines and media, down to its eventual saturation of the market in ever-recurring knock-offs of the originals. A trend's transition from the red carpet to the high street has speeded up over time with today's manufacturers able to turn it around in a matter of weeks rather than months. Although this fast fashion response is able to spread a trend quickly through its mass availability, it can also be the cause of its inevitable demise as that self-same popularity eventually takes the edge off its earlier appeal.

Here is a witty task that gives you the opportunity to spread the word (literally) of a fashion trend by building a visual alphabet relying upon a season's signature styles. Invention and creativity is key to your arrangements and always remember that sometimes less can be more.

1. Gather together a number of glossy magazines that promote the key components of a fashion season's trends. You could approach the task by sourcing Internet downloads, but hand collage will give you a better control.

2. It will be helpful to have a basic alphabet template as a reference when identifying your shapes and assembling your letters. A mix of upper and lower case will help give your trend alphabet diversity in appearance. Don't use an ornamental or decorative font that will detract from your collaged shapes. You want your letters to be easily recognized.

3. Start looking through your trend imagery to isolate fashion shapes that might work as single letters. Think of both upper- and lower-case lettering. Rotating the magazine might prompt some unusual suggestions. Remember that most alphabet letters will break down into simple horizontal, diagonal and vertical lines – this will allow you to build up new letters by mixing shapes.

4. Play around with your shapes to encapsulate a year's trend alphabet from A–Z and attach the results into your fashion sketchbook. If you want to finalize your entire alphabet into a similar font size, scan the final letters and re-size to a pre-selected dimension using computer software.

Right
Depending upon your wardrobe, an alternative approach would be to photograph tangible garment shapes to define your alphabet.

Opposite
Yvette Yang (2010)
Fashion Font 2010 Spring/Summer.

'Fashion is born by small facts, trends, or even politics, never by trying to make little pleats and furbelows, by trinkets, by clothes easy to copy, or by the shortening or lengthening of a skirt.'

Elsa Schiaparelli

Showcase 4

Name:
Dan Robenko
Nationality:
Israeli
Graduate:
Shenkar College of
Engineering, Design &
Art, Ramat Gan, Israel
Graduate Collection 2012:
'Under Surveillance'

'A sketchbook is a very important tool, not just for me, but for any practicing artist. I consider its main purpose is to visualize my ideas and help me catalogue my design process.

Ideas can sprout up suddenly from any place, any time, any source: media, movies, books, culture, arts, etc. As a fashion designer, I'm always trying to be sensitive to what is happening around me, and the world in general. When I have a basic idea, I try to look at it from different perspectives and develop my own vision and personal point of view. I start by gathering images and information that inspire me and to help establish a mood board for my new collection. My research always starts with Internet search engines because it is the fastest and most reliable way to find out information, new ideas and inspiration. The second stage is to visit the library in order to understand the connection between historical and present events.

For my 'Under Surveillance' collection I wanted to use the images I had collected to investigate and examine various ways of how to blur or hide an identity. The reality of current technology and the scope of the Internet mean that people can be easily monitored and deprived of their privacy. The research and preliminary sketches led me to places and ideas that I would never have considered. My initial ideas for the collection started with 'secret agents' that had become very popular in the 1950s. In comparison, I began to realize how much people today are exposed to surveillance and how easy it is to watch everyone. This made me think about what I would do to hide my own identity

so that I was able to express myself without any fear or control. When developing my menswear-collection silhouettes I was also inspired by the photo series of workers from 1950s taken by Irving Penn.

I began to map out a visual story before proceeding to the sketches that were the last stage prior to creating the collection. I prefer working on separate large sheets, such as A3, because I like to 'feel' the freedom it allows. It also allows me to attach large fabric swatches and better explain my design details and specifics. I then bring these individual sheets together to construct my sketchbook. The research I carried out and the images that I found help me to determine the right fabrication, build up the colour palette and produce my technical sketches for the garments.

My sketchbook proved invaluable in helping me to document the whole design process all the way through from research to its conclusion.'

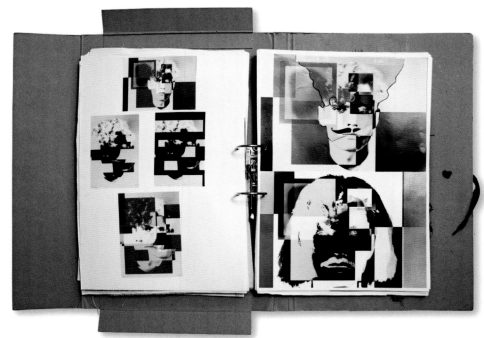

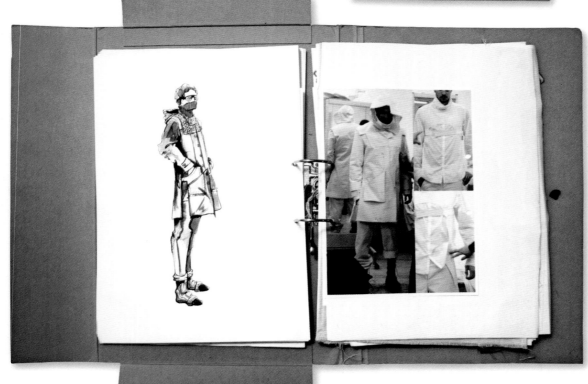

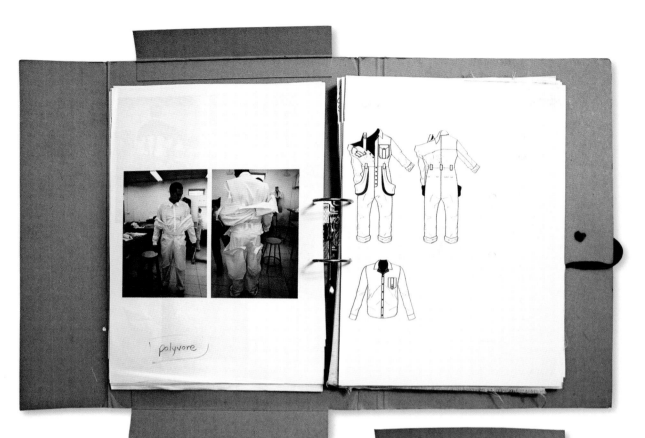

polyvore

CHAPTER 5
Design development: switching on your creativity

'My work is about ideas. If I had to define my philosophy in just a few words, it would be about an exploration, a journey, storytelling – it is a combination of these things with suggestions and proposals at the same time. It is a quest into certain areas and proposing a way of looking at something. I am very much an ideas person which my team help me to realise. I am not a one-man show. When you are someone trying to create an idea, you don't always have the means to make it practical first time round – the perpetual struggle of making a prototype and then making it real.'

Hussein Chalayan

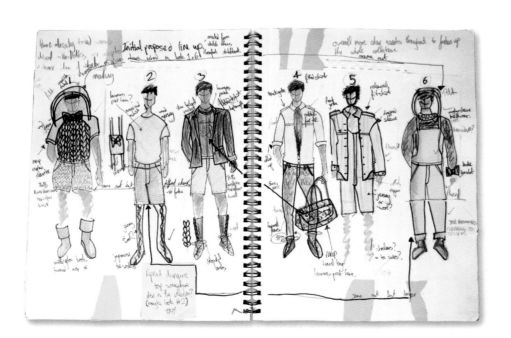

At the start of any design task, every designer is always faced with the daunting prospect of a blank canvas, white sheet of paper or empty screen. The potential of a clean slate is limitless but the undertaking can appear daunting. This is why the sketchbook is so useful to the process of design. It works like a visual crutch to support the whole process from the initial research through to the conclusion. It not only houses your research and reference material but it also charts your personal progress throughout the development of the design. It operates like a sounding board to test out ideas and check their viability in accordance with your concept and intentions.

Using the information already collated in your sketchbook, it is now time to devise a strategy that allows you to achieve your fashion designs. You will already have indications of the look and feel that you are after from the research you have collected in your sketchbook. You will have a clearer understanding of your customer and the marketplace. It is at this stage that your fashion designs will start to be directed towards prototypes and start to take physical shape.

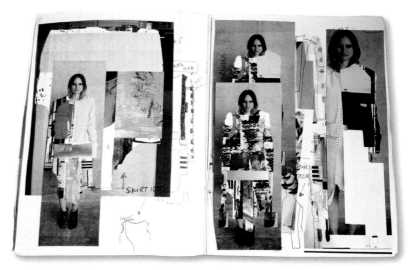

For most designers the process through which a project is developed is as rewarding as the final outcome itself. The challenge of developing the ideas from their concept stage and, via construction, through to their eventual realization, is as demanding as sourcing the initial research. It necessitates an inquiring mind that is able to match technical skills with a creative imagination. It is usually a very time-consuming activity, as ideas need sufficient time to evolve and develop. There is a need for continual analysis and evaluation as the process starts to expand, in order to ensure that the designs don't stray away from the original concept.

Your sketchbook will become the base camp for all your risk taking and experimentation. It is where you can return, to take stock of progress and further equip yourself for the next stage.

It is important that you keep your ideas flexible. Your vision might alter or adapt as you work through the design-development phase because of how your research is being put to use. It is crucial that you whole-heartedly believe in your intentions but you also need to be realistic about achieving them.

There are many factors that will begin to penetrate the design process that didn't seem important when it was just an idea in your head. As you start to make things happen, there will be innumerable questions for you to answer about physically achieving your goals in a way that still supports your original concept.

The design-development stage is the transition between your research and actual garments. It is the bridge between concept and reality. You will undertake to combine the key features from your earlier investigations – colour, silhouette, proportion, form, texture – with your personal interpretation for realizing your garment ideas based upon your primary and secondary research to give the designs their context.

The breadth of the concept is usually worked across a progression of related garments that work as individual looks but have a greater impact when see together as a unified collection.

Opposite, above
Kate Watson
(2010)

Opposite, below
Gwilym Lansley
(2011)

Above
Gemma Fanning (2012)

Below
Paul Kim (2012)
Design development is all about working out your design ideas so that you get the most from your research and experimentation by analysis and targeting your design concept.

A garment collection will vary depending on the size of the company and its product range. Range planning is a further consideration – how will the designer distribute the season's look across the collection when it is broken down into single items of clothing? A typical catwalk collection might consist of 30–40 separate outfits with an average of around three garments per look. This suddenly starts to mount up, with what could be up to 120 garments that need to be individually designed, patterned, fabricated and constructed on schedule each season. However, a collection is very rarely composed of completely independent items. Comparable with the collection's linked concept that binds the look together, the designer will use a strategy of repeating certain styles and features in alternative fabrics or garment ideas to condense the range down to more manageable proportions. A particular style line or intricate pattern detailing will re-surface throughout the collection, with the dual purpose of not only uniting the collection together as a overall look, but also moderating the need to return to the drawing board for each new design.

Sustaining an idea over a multitude of outfits is the testing point of any collection. The passion of the designer for their subject is expected, but the eventual designs will struggle if the research is insufficient to continually feed the concept as it develops. The sketchbook is an invaluable aid to this process, because as well as prompting future developments, it can also indicate where further investigation is necessary to support an idea.

An experienced designer can search through the sketchbook to sound out single ideas or by clustering a group of images together, generate new possibilities. A sketchbook should always be regularly pump-primed throughout the design development activity to keep it fresh and current. Updating and adding additional information to existing reference material as you proceed with your design development serves not only to archive your progress, but also help to stimulate alternative ideas.

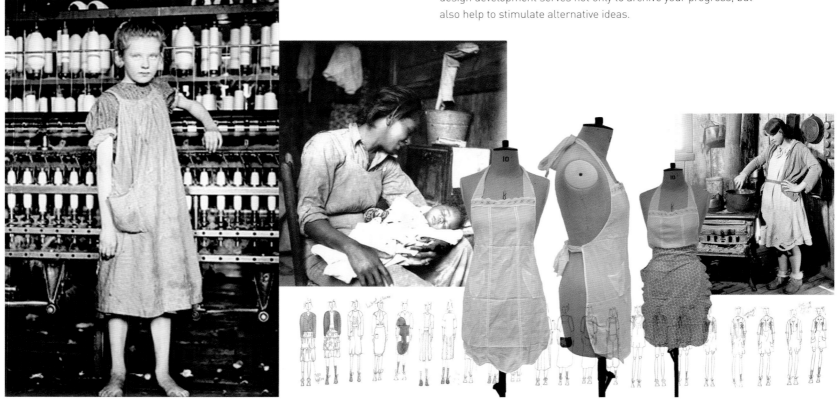

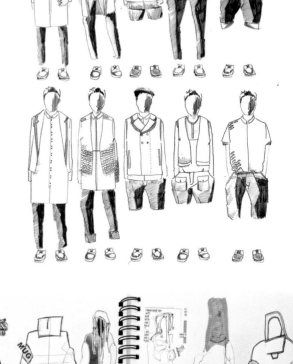

How the sketchbook pages are organized during design development will be a personal consideration for each individual designer. You might consider it imperative that the sketchbook adheres to a prearranged sequence showing a beginning, middle and end narrative that charts your development. It could be important for you to organize the layout of the information within a regimented and reiterated arrangement on each page to impart continuity within your sketchbook. You may feel that a more exposed and free assembly is better reflective of your own methodology for generating ideas. Ultimately, the structure is not the important factor – it is all about the sketchbook's content and its ability to strengthen your design development.

Although the design-development phase is the concluding design activity to be incorporated into your fashion sketchbook, prior to the actual assembly of your garment designs in fabric, it is undoubtedly the most important in the entire sequence of design. It represents the summation of all your design practice to date and should evidence your investigations into all the main components of your intended collection. Design development explains how you think and act. Every designer will value the content in different ways as a personal document of their own ability. The sketchbook also becomes an indispensable tool to explain your work to potential employers.

Whatever the end use, the design-development process in your sketchbook should involve these six considerations:

- Personal identity
- Hybrids
- Core items
- Prototypes
- Fabrication
- The line-up.

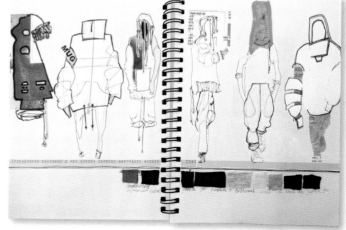

<u>Above</u>
Philippa Jenkins (2010)

<u>Below</u>
Kerrie Alexander (2012)
The sketchbook gives you a unique opportunity to flaunt your talent as a designer by revealing the process of your personal design development.

<u>Opposite</u>
Jessica Larcombe (2012)

Personality and identity

You have already learned how essential it is to gather key items of research and to evaluate all your ideas within a broader context. By now your sketchbook should be brimming with bountiful imagery and information struggling to be unconfined from its origin. The process of design development requires you to channel these findings towards defining your own personal concept.

You need to bring value to all these points of reference in as creative and original a way as possible. This is an opportunity to express your individuality as a designer and the message you want to communicate. This individual response is what assigns designers their distinctive characteristics. Similarly, the hang of a fabric, shape of a sleeve or embellishment of a neckline should challenge your abilities to disregard preconceptions and to generate new ideas within fashion design.

Design development is ultimately what makes your ideas stand out from those of your competitors. It is the distinctive and personal translation of your findings that accentuates your intentions and signals the conviction in your own interpretation of fashion. There should be a depth to the evolution of your design translation that adds weight and significance beyond the plain and obvious. By establishing a handwriting characteristic within your designs, you will be able to reposition your work away from the literal and available towards a more desirable and innovative creative level.

Your personal identity as a designer should be easily identifiable within the concept of your collection. Contemporary designers are branded because of the characteristics of their house style. Armani, Miyake and McQueen have as distinguishing a fashion identity as the paintings of Andy Warhol or the film scores of John Williams (b.1932). Establishing a personal identity is paramount for any new fashion designer. It is what makes you stand out in a very competitive market.

> 'When people ask if I have any advice to give about fashion, it's always the same: 'Follow your own pace, your own instincts, no matter what. You'll get it right.'
>
> André Leon Talley (b.1949)

Below
Alanna Kaye (2012)

As your personality drives your ideas towards identifying your design concept, it is important that you don't accept the first thought that come into your head without digging below its surface. Remember that once you have 'nailed your colours to the mast', you will have to live with the consequences of your decision. Glibly plucking a concept from the first image you find in your sketchbook is to be avoided. Never accept the glaringly obvious or take reference too literally – it will most likely already have been drained of all its design potential long ago. Also avoid jumping too eagerly onto the noticeable trend bandwagon stimulated by a new film or current media event. More than likely it will already have saturated the market before your designs hit the catwalk.

Once you have decided upon a suitable concept, you should learn to retell your theme like a musical *leitmotif* throughout the pages of your sketchbook. By keeping it always in play, it will help to reinforce the identity and underscore the personality of

Right
Alexander
Romaniewicz
(2012)

Far right
Linzi Reid
(2012)
'Autofluorescent
Anatomy'
Digging below
the surface
of your
research helps
to unearth
unchartered and
more personal
approaches to
develop towards
establishing
a personal
identity for
your work.

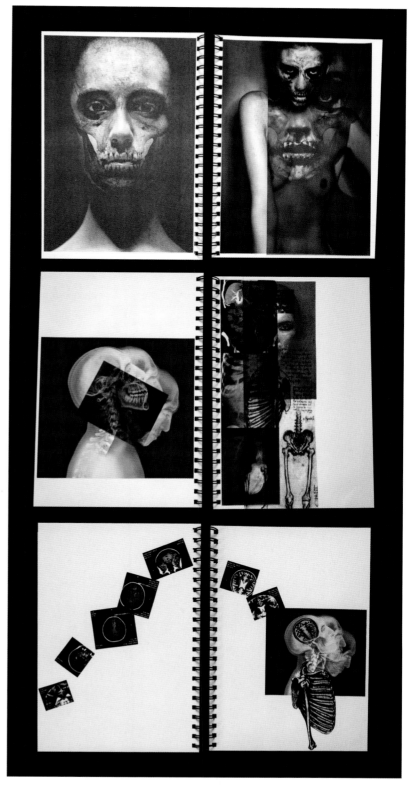

Hybrids

With your design concept now in place, you will be eager to extract ideas utilizing your assembled research. Adhering to the truism that 'from little acorns mighty oaks do grow', you need to begin the gradual process of shaping up the ideas that will eventually form your new collection, by testing out design after design in your sketchbook until you are happy with the result.

It is a significant period of evaluation and aesthetic judgement. You will already have amassed a quantity of interesting visual research from your investigations. It is now the stage to edit and refine all your findings by rearranging the pieces and putting them together with differing emphasis and appealing relationships.

Having pre-selected, for example, an architectural concept and pulled together an excess of supporting images and information,

'Inspiration is not a copy but a starting point, taking us somewhere new.'

Karl Lagerfeld

you will need to sieve through the research to highlight its unique features and original qualities as design stimuli. You might be using volume and scale, or the specific and detailing, as a springboard to inspiration. It may possibly be the texture of the building material itself or the composition of its assembly. Whatever the attributes that appeal to you, they now need to be articulated in fashion terms: the dramatic sweep of a cathedral buttress could be suggestive of a new shoulder line or silhouette; the regimentation of skyscraper windows could prompt a similar fragmentation to the body; the detailing around a doorframe might conjure up similar features or decoration for footwear or millinery. There will be innumerable possibilities within your research for design development, and it is down to you as a fashion designer, to extract and build on its potential through a process of trial and error.

Left
Nick Maloy (2010)
Adjusting your design ideas around a common shape is a convenient way to develop style alternatives that can be tested against each another for the most appealing design solution.

Opposite, above
Louise Bennetts (2012)

Opposite, below
Rosa Ng (2011)
Testing out multiple variations by hand is a quick method of achieving interesting hybrids away from your initial thoughts. Annotating your thoughts is also a useful sounding board to articulating your reasoning.

Drawing fashion flats is the best way to help you to expand your ideas. They should always be kept simple and clean to help you to realize the specifics of garment construction and design detailing. If they become too illustrative then the essentials of the design are easily lost within the artistic expression. Often a shorthand representation of the figure or none at all will suffice – the language of a flat is about the garment and not its style or image – that will happen later.

It is best to draw flats with a closer adherence to real proportions than in a fashion illustration, so that your design intentions are not influenced by an enhanced graphic representation. Because you will want to move swiftly from one idea to another it is often easier to make use of a figure croquis. This is a linear figure outline that can be placed underneath tracing paper or a layout pad so that you have a template to help you begin your design ideas quickly without having to worry about establishing a figure each time. The repetition of the figure shape also helps you to reflect upon the best solution when you come to compare like with like. Style and construction lines, including details of decorative stitching, should always be indicated to add integrity to the designs. These will eventually evolve into the working drawings of your garments and are better kept diagrammatic to explain the technical composition of the clothes. For quick design generation, execution by hand is very accommodating, although to reach industry standard, flats and technical specification drawings would usually be prepared using software programmes like Adobe Illustrator, Freehand or CorelDRAW.

Make the most of your flat drawings to reveal all the hidden design elements by repeating style lines and design information over and over again from an assortment of alternative viewpoints. A good designer should be able to rework plenty of fresh ideas from a single source of inspiration: it might be as simple as adjusting the hem or sleeve lengths to generate shifts in proportion; lowering or raising a neckline to challenge convention or the introduction of seaming or dart lines within the overall silhouette to draw attention to a specific body area.

Never give up after the first attempt – learn to produce large quantities of style tasters in your sketchbooks. When you are satisfied with your design suggestions you can start to pre-select the superior ideas that will be utilized in your definitive design sequence.

It is important that you consider the 3D aspect of your ideas in your flats. Although your drawing will inevitably have a defining edge at the left and right of the body silhouette, in reality there is no such boundary. Don't assume that everything you design will automatically contain a side seam or even a centre front or back opening. Even though you are drawing two-dimensionally you need to be conscious that you are actually designing a 3D shape.

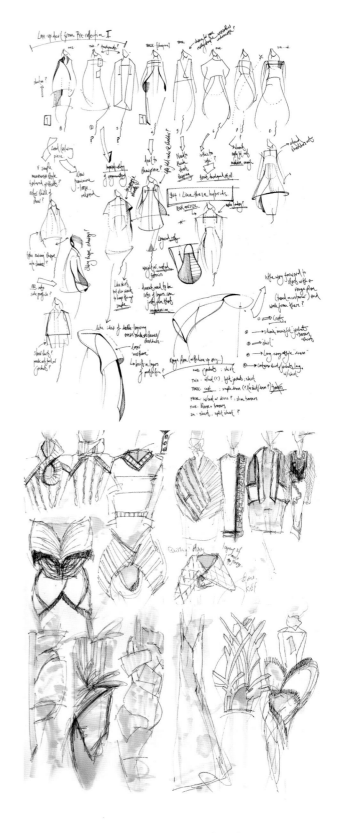

Core items

'It's a new era in fashion - there are no rules.'

Alexander McQueen

Your knowledge of the fashion calendar and investigative shop reports will already have set the wheels of design direction in motion. It is important to have determined the season and target customer before you begin to assemble your final line-up of designs. With your market guidelines in place you can now connect your varied research design experiments into garments under the umbrella of your concept theme. It is essential that a designer's personal concept should always remain pure and focused and not become superficially inflated or weakened when it is expanded across a range or collection.

sailor fuku
Black sailor

concept
The symbol of youth
puberty
Growth

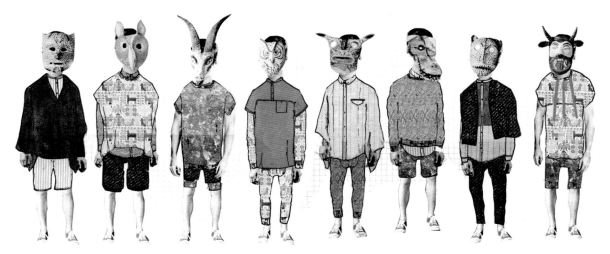

To begin with you need to establish the core items that will encapsulate your intended range. There will be a need for diversification within the selection to avoid monotony, but there is also a requirement for cohesion under your concept theme. Obviously there will be different compositional requirements depending upon your choice of market. The considerations for a designer menswear range will be different to those for budget fashion teen group. Not only in the specific composition of the garments, but in their function as part of a fashion wardrobe.

How you achieve the bond throughout the range will depend upon how you translate your research and formulate your look. Most collections will consist of separates, and this mix-and-match methodology to building up an image is identical, whether it is for day or eveningwear collections. A daywear wardrobe will usually contain more individual items than with eveningwear, but the same considerations towards balance and composition are critical for the success of either look. Specialist areas such as sportswear are as much about function as image and careful attention needs to be paid to the advances in new technology to keep abreast of developments in smart design.

The number of pieces in a collection can vary from as few as 30 to well over 100. A new designer or student will usually rely upon the impact and originality of their designs rather than volume to capture attention. A typical fashion-student collection is usually centered around six catwalk looks.

It is often useful to determine a key signature look for the collection: a preferred image that seems to sum up all that your range is about in terms of image, colour, fabric and cut. This should be capable of grabbing the attention of the press and buyers and confidently scale the editorial headlines.

Just as it is easy to immediately recall the signature looks of fashion's glitterati – Suzy Menkes's (b.1943) architectural coiffure or Karl Lagerfeld's ponytail and fan – you need something that could travel with your collection from its design through to retail and give it an eye-catching, original identity.

Opposite
Katsura Funaki (2012)
The core items of your collection should be a summary of your design concept expressed in suitably striking imagery to give impact to the originality of your designs.

Above
Faye
Oakenfull
(2012)

Right
Alexander
Romaniewicz
(2012)

Prototypes

The majority of the design development within your sketchbook will initially consist of hand-drawn experiments to do with shape and line. It is equally important to match your sketched ideas with 3D prototypes and sampling. By alternating between the 2D and 3D, you will not only be able to put your flats physically to the test, but the activity will spark new ideas that you would not have been aware of when drawing them out simply as lines on paper. This flexible to-ing and fro-ing is a necessary component of design development. It ensures that you will gain the best from your research when translated alongside your design concept.

Experimenting with fabric on a dress stand is the globally accepted method of converting 2D ideas into 3D form. This process is usually called toiling or moulage. Although a calico or muslin substitute replaces the final fabric choice at this experimental stage, when creating a toile it is important to use a fabric that has similar properties to your intended choice. An unyielding cotton canvas will not be able to replicate the qualities of a stretch jersey or knitted fabric; similarly if you intend to use leather, don't test out your ideas in fine cheesecloth.

Although fabrication is an important consideration when toiling, references to the colour choice are not as imperative. By working in an unbleached fabric, it is easy to mark up your construction lines and clearly identify any faults. The fashion designer works like a sculptor directly onto the mannequin, often disregarding conventional patterning aids. Armed with only a mouthful of pins and brandishing a pair of shears, a skilled designer can work magic by draping a length of calico against the dress stand.

Starting with straightforward shaping and manipulation, garment ideas can be reworked from your pre-selected design sketches, by simply folding, pleating or gathering the calico to replicate your concepts. It is often rewarding to explore a basic shape from your research and apply it to the dress stand to see how it reacts to the contours of the body form. Drawing a certain effect may work on paper, but it is the extra considerations that you need to apply when it becomes a reality that test your imagination as a creative designer.

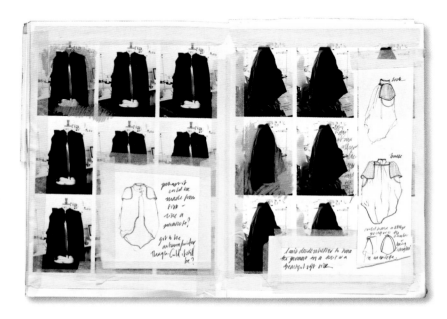

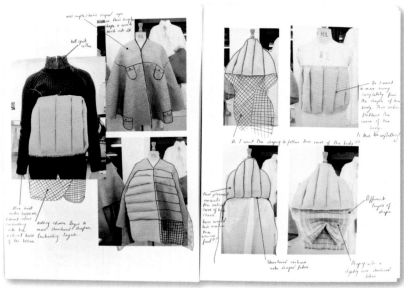

You need to evaluate continually your fabric experimentation and top-up your design development sketches from your findings. It is a constant two-way process of exchange and personal negotiation. Pay particular attention to the smaller details that are inevitably lost when you are working out ideas at a reduced scale on paper. You will soon begin to appreciate that in addition to translating your sketched ideas into the round, working on the dress stand will also prompt avenues to explore that you were unable to capture with just a 2D line.

Because of the symmetry of the human body, it is customary to begin to toile against half of the dress stand, although this more appropriate for tailored and structured garments. This process becomes a useful shorthand when marking up pattern pieces from the calico toiles by ensuring a mirrored left and right within the finished garment. To understand how your full garment will look, it is always necessary to complete a prototype in full rotation.

It is paramount that you record your experimentation to assist in your deliberations during design development. Many of your manipulations will be momentary considerations and completely alter with the insertion of another pin or fold of fabric. Hand drawing is usually replaced at this stage by capturing your 3-D progress directly on to film. Photography is ideal since it offers an instant record of the real-life rendition and doesn't slow down your stand work by interrupting your thought processes. Photography also enables you swiftly to document your garment from different angles or zoom in on a particular detail. The introduction of photographs of your toiles alongside the design flats in your sketchbook acknowledges the thoroughness and consideration within the design development of your personal concept.

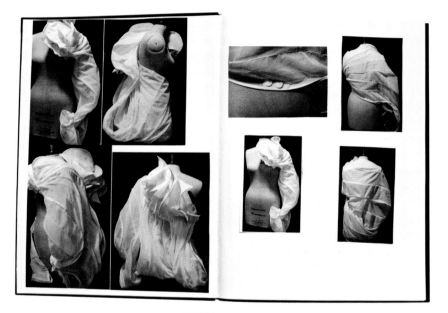

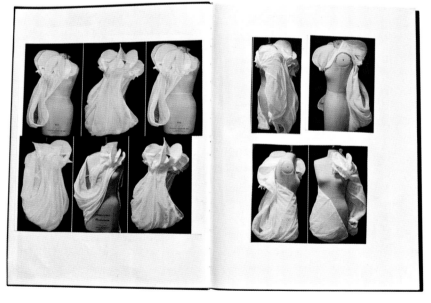

Opposite, left
Hâf Evans (2012)

Opposite, right
Emma Hardstaff (2012)

Above and below
Alena Johnson (2011)
Your sketchbook allows you to move between your 2-D and 3-D experiments, which should be continuously recorded and analyzed throughout design development.

Fabrication

Fabric for a fashion designer is the equivalent of marble to a sculptor or paint to an artist. It is the medium all designers work with to achieve their fashion objectives.

'Clothes create a wordless means of communication that we all understand.'

Katharine Hamnett

A fashion designer's artistic expression and judgment is constantly put to the test during the design development phase and the correct media is the dominant factor underpinning the entire process. Consequently, fabrication becomes critical in the design development, and remains a fundamental consideration for fashion designers when striving to achieve a physical appearance that tallies with their initial design ideas.

Although the fabric will also introduce texture and colour within the look, its foremost function is to achieve the garments' shape and volume through the properties of its distinctive construction, and the effects of its handle and use.

Being too subjective when choosing fabric should be avoided. The instant appeal of a certain fabric might have the requisite 'wow' factor, but you need to ask yourself whether it also has the characteristics that will support your design. Does it have the right fibre content and construction? Does it drape well? Is it too heavy or too flimsy? Do its functional properties work with or against your design intentions?

A rudimentary understanding of the properties of different fabrics is key to obtaining the best from both your design and the cloth itself. Trying to create a severe, sculptural silhouette from a naturally draping fabric would require excessive understructure and ultimately look contrived and artificial. Likewise, using fake fur to show off intricate patterning and multi-seaming details would defeat the objective, because the subtlety of the style lines would become lost within the fabric's dense texture.

<u>Left</u>
Philippa Jenkins (2010)
Fabrication is not only key for the shape and hang of garments but it also introduces colour and texture into your designs.

Moving between your sketchbook flats and the outcome of fabrication experiments on the dress stand will allow you to integrate the two activities so that you do not fall into the trap of creating design ideas while unaware of the fabric's properties and potential. In the same way that an extraordinary fabric will require vision and careful manipulation to build upon its inherent qualities, a garment flat is only as good as the creative foresight that can eventually transform it into a viable garment, and that requires knowledge and information about fabrication. In knitwear, a garment's design and fabric structure are already linked because they develop simultaneously as the fashioned fabric builds to create the definitively shaped design.

Both the season and market segmentation will also inform your fabric choice. An autumn/winter wardrobe will typically require heavier fabrics than a spring/summer collection. Cloth properties and finishes also need to be considered. Outerwear that is not weatherproof would obviously detract from its suitability for the mass garment market. However, don't be afraid of challenging the source of a variety of specialist fabrics by altering its end usage. Appropriating a furnishing fabric into fashion, or selecting a performance fabric or industrial cloth for its aesthetic properties rather than original function, is not necessarily a negative gamble. Ringing the changes in the convention of fabric application will certainly draw attention to your designs.

It might be appropriate to your design concept to experiment with the fabric's natural properties to achieve a more relevant appearance. Distressing a fabric, or printing across its surface, are easy, do-it-yourself approaches to personalizing your fabrication successfully in support of the look you are after. The requisite consideration for fashion designers is whether the selected fabric is fit for its end purpose, either practically or artistically.

It is equally necessary to bear in mind the practicalities of obtaining sufficient fabric to meet your needs and its eventual financial cost. Any constraints over fabric supply could detrimentally impact on your overall look: it would normally be unconstructive to play safe and restrict yourself to a single cloth and supplier unless your eventual market dictated a primary cloth composition as with jeans and denim. It is more likely for your garment designs to be reliant upon several sources for the fabric provision. Not only will the fabric be from different manufacturers, it will probably not even be from the same country. Ensuring that cloth is ready and available when you need it can prove a logistical problem even for the most seasoned designer.

Also, with fabrication, comes the benefit of introducing colour and texture within the collection. Along with the concept and silhouette, these attributes will permeate throughout your designs and contribute to the cohesion of the entire look. It is impractical to select fabric for your garments without taking into account its surface colour and likewise colour is only made visible in your designs through the fabric choice. Remember that the density or texture of a fabric will alter a shade or hue of exactly the same colour, and that devising a colour palette for your designs independently from the fabric choice may leave you frustrated by the non-availability of the eventual selection.

<u>Right</u>
Georgia Smith (2012)

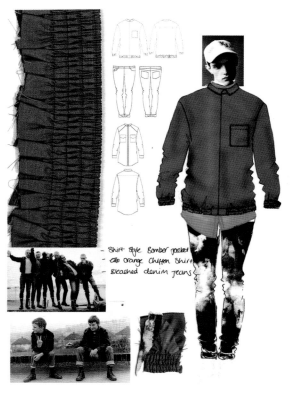

The line-up: decision time

'The secret of fashion is to surprise and never to disappoint.'

Edward Bulwer-Lytton (1803-73)

Once you are convinced that all the components of your collection are in place, you need to conclude the design development phase by preparing an illustrated line-up of all your intended garments. This will give you the opportunity to peruse your proposed collection to check if it lives up to your design concept.

It is crucial to use objective judgement, and rationally consider whether your line-up represents a suitably original and unique statement about contemporary fashion. Does it stand apart from the rest? Is the design concept confidently expressed and well dispersed throughout the full range of garments? Does the collection include enough content and detailing to reflect the range?

There may have been a design or garment that you struggled with throughout the development process and are still reluctant to lose even though it is now redundant. Subjectivity must not be allowed to sway your verdict over its inclusion. At times there will be a very simple idea that you arrived at almost effortlessly that might work better in the line-up, rather than an over-complex construction that was technically demanding and very time consuming. Your heart should never be allowed to rule your head in concluding your evaluation.

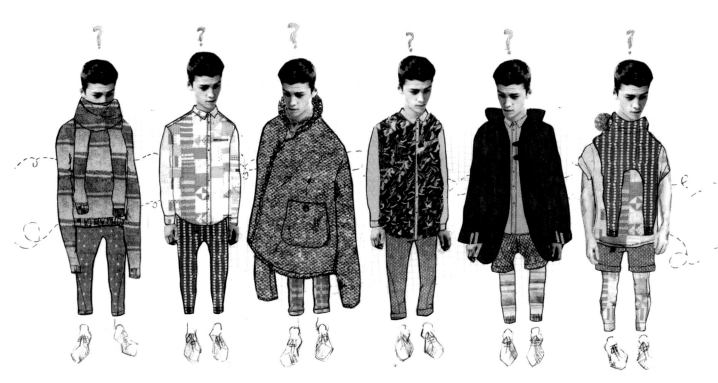

Left
Faye Oakenfull (2012)

Opposite
Tiffany Baron (2012) The final line-up needs careful consideration to fuse your design concept with your intended target market.

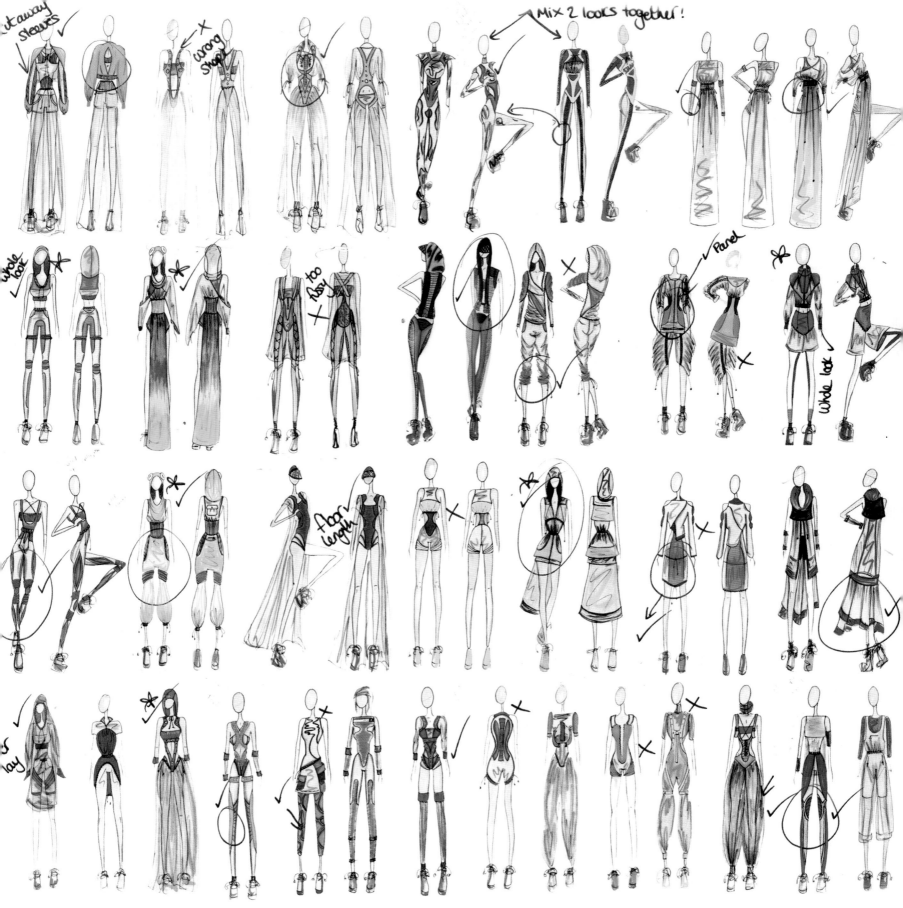

It is key to generate
a cohesive look
to your line-up,
through fabrication,
colour or shape that
provides variety
within the individual
components that
operate under the
umbrella of your
design concept.

If you consider that your designs require further clarification,
introducing your flats where appropriate within the line-up's
composition will support your illustrated designs by the addition
of their more technical language.

Most of the drawings made during design development will have been carried out as quick-fire ideas to test out shapes, styles and silhouettes. Colour tests will have been mixed then trialled, and fabric types introduced by attaching cut samples of actual cloth. It is now time to preview your final selection of ideas as a unified collection by gathering together all of your finally approved designs across a single spread in your sketchbook.

An illustrated line-up represents the synthesis of your design concept as researched and developed throughout your sketchbook. It is like the visual *dramatis personae* of your collection. Whereas the generation of ideas and assemblies of fabrication have been carried out with more concern for the actual design development than any aesthetic considerations of the marks on the page, the final line-up deserves a more considered approach to its appearance in your sketchbook.

Using a more illustrative treatment to represent your designs is a beneficial way of attracting attention. You might want to build upon characteristics discovered during your initial research or choose a style more akin to your design concept. By making use of a more distinctive and personal illustrative style you will be able to strengthen the individuality of your line-up's representation.

Below
Alexander Lamb (2011)

Showcase 5

Name:
Jousianne Propp
Nationality:
German/American
Graduate:
Manchester School of Art, UK
Graduate Collection 2012:
'Technoligion'

'The ideas for my work usually come from abstract sources. Literature, science, history, something on the news or new technology can all inspire me. It is often the concepts behind these things that excite me more than anything, and the first step in my work is usually trying to translate these into something visual. Ideas and concepts don't physically exist, and my sketchbook is the place where I can figure out how to turn them into images and shapes.

I usually work on loose sheets of paper because I like to be able to move them around, putting different pages next to each other all the time to form new ideas. Drawing next to or on top of my research images and overlapping layers of visual and textural information creates a very organic flow of ideas. It ends

up like a very coherent story with drawings, photographs, notes, Post-it notes, fabrics and collages. My graduate collection work explores the friction between science and religion – two areas of human endeavour and existence that continually fascinate me. The shapes and patterns are inspired by the sensation of awe and veneration induced by both religious imagery and scientific understanding. Using the principles of 3D printing technology, I have digitally 'dissected' bodies and reformed them into new shapes – evolving them into live, moving cathedrals.

The sketchbook pages here show how my research and observational drawings immediately translate into ideas for garments or textures on the body. Much of my sketchbook includes scruffy sketches full of notes and bits of fabric, but the layout and dynamic of the page are also very important to me, as they can directly inspire the proportions or dynamic of a garment.'

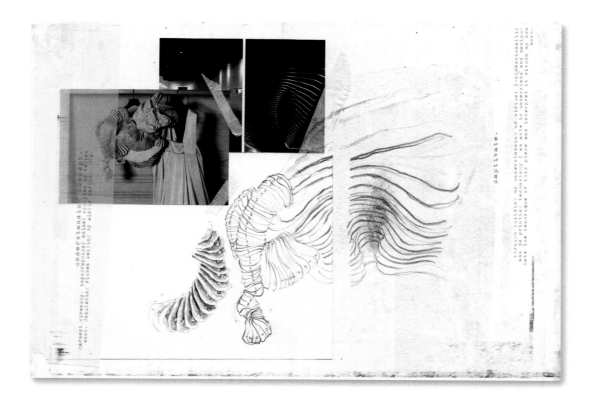

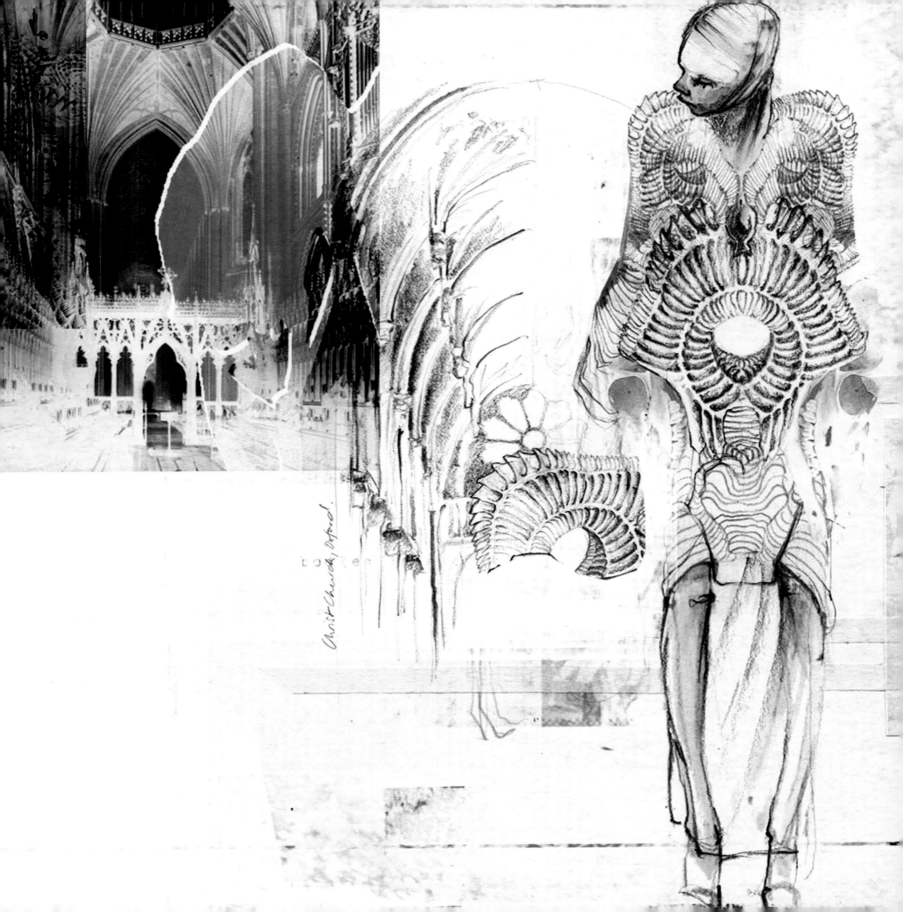

Christ Church, Oxford.

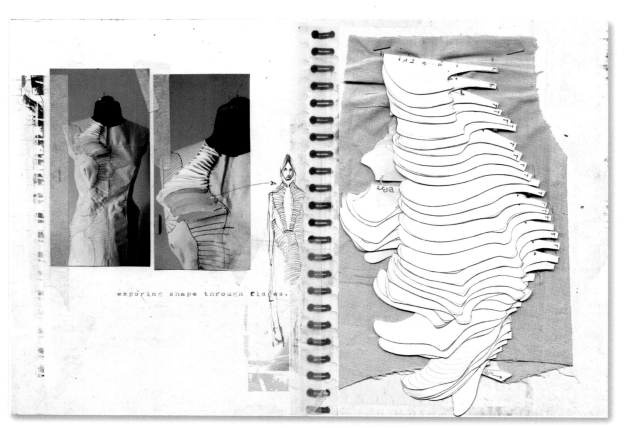

exploring shape through ridges.

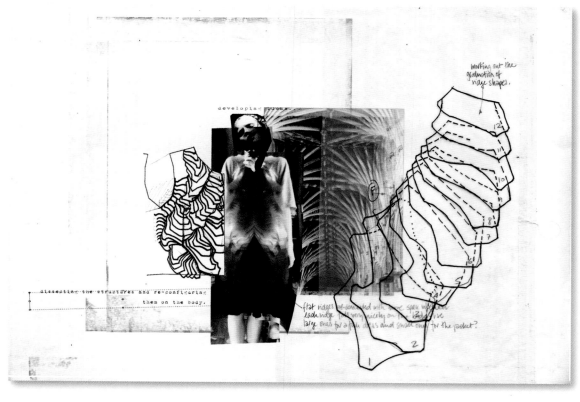

developing forms

dissecting the structures and re-configuring them on the body.

working out the graduation of ridge shapes.

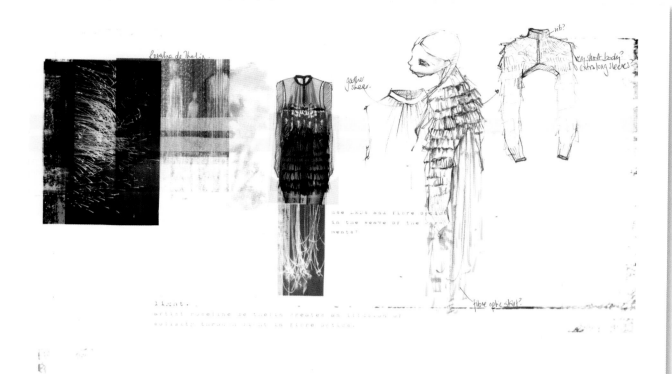

Rosaline de Thelin

gather
sheer.

nb?

very sheer body?
extra long sleeves?

fibre optic skirt?

light.

use this and fibre optic
in the weave of the gar-
ments?

artist Rosaline de Thelin creates an illusion of
infinity through the use of fibre optics.

buried strong
at the edge

combine the stiwhile structure with
the organic stiff spacer mesh shapes?

interfolded
pleats?

shape, print on acetate.
test (see photographic file)

building complexity through simplicity.
the modular-based structure allows for
endless transformation.

YOUR TEN-POINT CHECKLIST TO SUCCESSFUL DESIGN DEVELOPMENT:

1. Did you carry out sufficient research to instigate the design process and have you extracted the best from it?

2. Is there sufficient depth to the design concept and your own creative interpretation?

3. Have you considered the demands of your season, market level and target customer?

4. How successfully has colour, texture and detail been applied throughout your garments?

5. Do your designs reflect an understanding of social needs and contemporary values?

6. Is there a convincing aesthetic and visual impact to your designs?

7. Do your designs say something new about fashion?

8. Have you taken risks or has it become a compromise?

9. Does the final line-up showcase your personal strengths as a fashion designer?

10. Have you fulfilled yourself creatively?

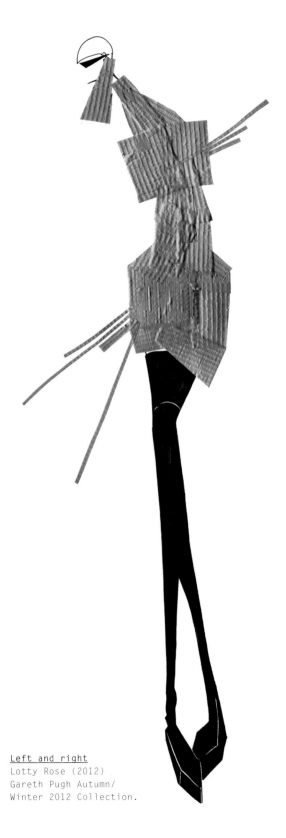

Left and right
Lotty Rose (2012)
Gareth Pugh Autumn/
Winter 2012 Collection.

CONTACT DETAILS

Kerrie Alexander
kerriealexander@hotmail.co.uk
kerriealexander.blogspot.com
www.kerriealexander.com

Kayleigh Jean Allen
kayleighjeanallen@gmail.com
www.kayleighjean.com
billiejean44.blogspot.com

Talisa Almonte
talisaalmonte@yahoo.com

Nicola Amodio
nicola.amodio.fashion@gmail.com
www.nicolaamodio.co.uk

Sandra Azwan
sandraazwan@gmail.com
bysandraazwan.blogspot.com

Felicity Baggett
felicitybaggett@gmail.com

Tiffany Baron
tiffanybaron@hotmail.co.uk
tiffanynfashion.blogspot.co.uk
www.artsthread.com/pv/tiffanybaron

Jade Barrett
jade.barrett@hotmail.com
jade-barrett-digital.tumblr.com
jade-barrett-digital.wix.com/jade-barrett-digital

Maggie Bone
fashion_enquiries@bathnes.gov.uk
www.fashionmuseum.co.uk

Maria-Anna Bena
m.a.bena@hotmail.com

Louise Bennetts
bennettslouise@gmail.com
www.cargocollective.com/louisebennetts
www.louisebennettscollection.tumblr.com

Avanti Bidikar
avanti@bidikar.com
www.avanti.bidikar.com

Claire Billington
claire.v.billington@gmail.com
clairebillington.wix.com/fashionportfolio

Yuliya Bogdanova
y.bogdanova@yahoo.com
www.yuliyabogdanova.com

Laura Bowler
laura.bowler@live.com

Amanda Brown
amandabrown83@msn.com

Lloyd Burchill
lloyd@flamingpear.com
www.flickr.com/photos/lloydb

Matteo Busanna
matteo.busanna@yahoo.it
www.matteobusanna.com

Julie Campbell
juliebeafraid@gmail.com
www.facebook.com/afraidbeafraid

Filomena Cavallaro
memy.cavallaro@libero.it
www.filomenacavallaro.it

Milda Cergelyte
info@mimicfashion.co.uk
www.mimicfashion.co.uk

Eugene Czarnecki
geneczar@aol.com
www.eugeneczarnecki.com

Conrad James Dawney
houseofslater@gmail.com
www.houseofslater.com

Beckie Docherty
beckie.docherty@hotmail.co.uk

Klaus Dolle
klausdolle@gmail.com
www.klausdolle.eu

Hannah Dowds
hannahdowds@hotmail.co.uk
hannahdowds.carbonmade.com

Shabria Dowley
shabiradowley@hotmail.com
info@shabiradowley.com
www.shabiradowley.com

Rebecca Dring
rebeccadring7@gmail.com
imaginarymillionaire.blogspot.co.uk

Misha Lucie Hannah Edwards
mishamezzone@gmail.com
mishamezzone.blogspot.co.uk

Hâf Evans
haf@haf.me.uk
www.haf.me.uk

Gemma Fanning
gemmamaireadfanning@gmail.com
www.gemmafanning.com
gemmafanning.tumblr.com
www.lookk.com/gemma-fanning

Clifford Faust
cliffordfaust57@gmail.com
www.cliffordfaust.com

Florentsya
florentsya@yahoo.com
www.wix.com/florentsya/florentsya

Julien Foucher
blomki@lebloc.net
http://www.lebloc.net

Katsura Funaki
smsmk5f@yahoo.co.jp

Eugenia Alejos Garrido
eugenialejos@gmail.com
www.eugenialejos.com
www.eugenialejos.blogspot.com

Thomas P. Gates
tgates@kent.edu

www.kent.edu/library/about/branches/fashion/index.cfm

Ekaterina Gerasimova
katrina-star@list.ru
www.katia-design.com

Geoffry Gertz
geoffry@sparked.biz
digitaldesigntherapy.com

George Gozum
inquire@gozum.com
www.gozum.com

Jack Grange
jack@jackgrange.co.uk
www.jackgrange.co.uk

Maureen Guido
Viridian5@aol.com
www.flickr.com/photos/26154094@N03

Jade Elizabeth Hannam
jadehannam85@hotmail.com

Emma Hardstaff
emma.hardstaff@network.rca.ac.uk
www.cargocollective.com/emmahardstaff

Rebecca Head
rebecca.head09@hotmail.co.uk
www.1in600.tumblr.com

Jessie Holmes
jessholmes5@hotmail.com
www.jessieholmes.com

Jenny H. Hong
jennyhong97@gmail.com
www.jennyheej.blogspot.co.uk

Xiaoping Huang (Fiona)
info@xiaopinghuang.com
www.xiaopinghuang.com

Philippa Jenkins
pip.jenkins@hotmail.com

Alena Kudera Johnson
alenakudera@hotmail.co.uk
info@alenakuderajohnson.com
www.alenakuderajohnson.com

Natalie Johnson
natalie_johnson_250390@hotmail.co.uk
artsthread.com/p/nataliejohnson

Chloe Jones
chloevictoriajones@gmail.com

Yuka Kanagawa
Represented by Fashion Illustration
Laboratory, Bunka Gakuen University, A137
3-22-1Yoyogi, Shibuya-ku, Tokyo, 151-8523,
Japan
ppppp_kanagawa@yahoo.co.jp

Studio Codex (Mendie Karagantcheff)
contact@studiocodex.nl
www.studiocodex.nl

Alanna Kaye
alannakaye@hotmail.co.uk
www.alannakaye.co.uk

Paul Kim
Paul.yk.kim@gmail.com

Julia Krantz
info@juliakrantz.com
www.juliakrantz.com

Alexander Lamb
alexander.lamb@hotmail.co.uk
www.tumblr.com/tagged/alexander+lamb

Rachel Lamb
racheljadelamb@live.com
http://cargocollective.com/racheljade

Gwilym Lansley
gwilymlansley@hotmail.com
www.gwilymlansley.co.uk
gxlansley.blogspot.com

Jessica Larcombe
jess.k.larcombe@googlemail.com
cargocollective.com/JessicaLarcombe

Anna Larson
anna_larson@hotmail.co.uk
thisannajosephine.blogspot.co.uk

Kayleigh MacBeth
kayleighmacbeth@hotmail.co.uk
kayleighmacbeth.blogspot.co.uk,
kayleighmacbeth.weebly.com

Nick Maloy
nick.maloy@gmail.com
www.coroflot.com/nmaloy

Hila Martuzana
martuzana@yahoo.com
www.coroflot.com/martuzana

Christopher C. McDaniel
cmcdaniel@gmail.com
www.flickr.com/photos/mcdanielism

Danielle Meder
finalfashion@gmail.com
www.finalfashion.ca

Fay Millard
fay_millard@live.co.uk
missfaysfashion.tumblr.com

Meagan Morrison
mmillustrations@gmail.com
www.meaganmorrison.com
travelwritedraw.blogspot.com

Eleanor Mountfort
hello@eleanormountfort.co.uk
www.eleanormountfort.co.uk

Hollie Louise Newton
hollienewton@hotmail.co.uk
hollienewton.blogspot.co.uk

Rosa Ng
ngk.rosa@gmail.com
www.underqc.com

Faye Oakenfull
faye.oakenfull@network.rca.ac.uk
www.artsthread.com/p/fayeoakenfull

Aušra Osipavičiūtė
aography@gmail.com
www.aography.com

Elvan Otgen
mail@elvanotgen.com
www.elvanotgen.com

Catherine Patterson
cat.patterson@yahoo.com
showtime.arts.ac.uk/cat88

Jousianne Propp
j.propp@hotmail.co.uk

Outi Pyy
outsapop.com@gmail.com
www.outsapop.com

Linzi Helen Reid
linzi.reid88@gmail.com
www.linzi-helen-reid.blogspot.com

Emily Rickard
ejrickard@gmail.com

Dan Robenko
dan.robenko@gmail.com
www.behance.net/danrobenko

Liliana Rodriguez
lulugaia01@yahoo.co.uk
www.lilianarodriguez.co.uk

Alexander Romaniewicz
aromaniewicz@yahoo.co.uk
therebelsescape.wordpress.com

Lotty Rose
rose_cf@hotmail.co.uk
www.lottyroseillustration.carbonmade.com
www.lottyrose.tumblr.com

National Museum of Singapore
nhb_nm_corpcomms@nhb.gov.sg
www.nationalmuseum.sg

Georgia Smith
georgia.l.p.smith@gmail.com

Sreejith Sreekumar
jithu.srijith@gmail.com
www.coroflot.com/baldheadhottea
www.baldheadhottea.blogspot.com

Rebecca Scarlett Stant
rebecca.scarlett@yahoo.co.uk
http://www.artsthread.com/p/
rebeccascarlettstant

Sumbal Tariq
eternalwings@hotmail.co.uk
soomify.tumblr.com

Christabel Bryony Taylor
christabel.taylor@googlemail.com
www.christabeltaylor.blogspot.com

Lucy Jane Taylor
lucyjane.taylor@hotmail.co.uk

Carolina Turner
info@carolinaturner.com
www.carolinaturner.com

Joel Janse van Vuuren
info@joeljansevanvuuren.com
www.joeljansevanvuuren.com

Charlotte Vieilledent
charlotte_vieilledent@hotmail.com
www.coroflot.com/charlottevieilledent

Olga Vokálová
info@olgavokalova.com
www.olgavokalova.com

Kate Watson
kmwatson.01@gmail.com
theloop.com.au/katewatson

Kelly Wenrick
kellywenrick@gmail.com

Carla Liane Williams
carlawilliams.design@gmail.com
cargocollective.com/carlawilliams

Ross Williams
rossdavidwilliams@hotmail.co.uk
www.rossdavidwilliams.com

Samme Williams
samme@sammewilliams.com
www.sammewilliams.com

Yvette Yang
yv@nmyv.com
www.fashion-font.com

Quinn Zhu
soleda29@yahoo.com.cn
www.chukquinn.blogspot.com